D0519103

GRAEME SOUNESS –
A MANAGER'S DIARY

GRAEME
SOUNESS
A MANAGER'S DIARY

GRAEME SOUNESS
with
Ken Gallacher

MAINSTREAM
PUBLISHING

© Graeme Souness and Ken Gallacher, 1989

All rights reserved

Reprinted 1989

First published in Great Britain 1989 by
MAINSTREAM PUBLISHING COMPANY (EDINBURGH) LTD
7 Albany Street
Edinburgh EH1 3UG

ISBN 1 85158 224 X (cloth)

No part of this book may be reproduced or transmitted in any form or by
any other means without the permission in writing from the publisher,
except by a reviewer who wishes to quote brief passages in connection with
a review written for insertion in a magazine, newspaper or broadcast.

British Library Cataloguing in Publication Data
Souness, Graeme
  Graeme Souness: a manager's diary.
  1. Scotland, Football League football, Clubs, Management
  Biographies
  I. Title II. Gallacher, Ken
  796.334′63′0924

  ISBN 1-85158-224-X

Typeset in 11 on 13pt Times by Blackpool Typesetting Services Ltd,
Blackpool.
Printed in Great Britain by Billings & Sons, Worcester.

Contents

1

The Signing That Stunned Soccer

No signing in the history of Scottish soccer caused an impact as great as when Mo Johnston joined Rangers in July 1989. It was the bombshell of the century – a signing which ended the unwritten and unspoken ban on Catholic players which had been in place at Ibrox for most of the club's existence. And it had further controversy added to it because only two months earlier it had seemed that the World Cup star was set to return to Parkhead to play for Rangers' oldest rivals, Celtic.

When Graeme Souness was first appointed as manager of Rangers a little over three years earlier he had pledged that he would sign any player of any denomination if it was to strengthen the team. He had tried previously to sign Ray Houghton, a Catholic player who later joined Liverpool. He had insisted that he would break the barrier and those who know him realised that this single-minded man would do it some day. But it would happen only when the player involved was a man he thought would add lustre to the side. Souness would not look beyond the player's ability. That would always have to be the yardstick for any signing he made.

But, of course, when the news broke it did so with all the spectacle and drama which Souness has brought with him to the club. One of his trademarks as a manager is his capacity to produce the unexpected and to win headlines. Here he did both in a way that few people in football will ever match.

In the years previously he had negotiated a series of big money transfers from the English First Division, reversing a trend which had always in the past seen Scottish clubs being plundered for their talented players by the clubs in the south. Souness altered that. He also brought a swagger to Rangers, and a glamour which saw crowds in the Premier League grow season after season. As every other country in Europe saw gates decline the Premier League in Scotland flourished – and a great deal of that was down to Souness and Rangers. It remains the same today and signings such as the Johnston one help to add lustre to the League. Here in his diary Souness unfolds the drama behind the Johnston bid and his reasons for moving as he did. And when he did.

1 July 1989

Celtic have now announced officially that they have ended their interest in Mo Johnston. The whole business has dragged on for six long weeks now and finally it's over. They have lost a good player. It also signifies, though, that Johnston is now available for other teams to buy. Nantes don't want him to stay in France and while other clubs on the continent, particularly in France, have said they would buy him, he has suggested he would like to return to Scottish football.

I wonder if he would come to us? Now there is a thought! He would strengthen us up front, give us another option, and he has improved a lot since he went to play in France. I have been really impressed with him when he has been playing for Scotland in the World Cup games. His scoring record at that level was exceptional last season. I must talk this one over with Walter.

3 July 1989

I sat down with Walter at Ibrox today and when I mentioned Mo to him it took just seconds for him to agree that he would be a tremendous signing for Rangers. The question of religion wasn't brought up immediately. I knew there were problems in that area but my first thought was only for the boy's footballing ability. That was the priority. In fact, that is always the way we approach signings. You examine the player's ability and then you think about how he would fit into the team and what kind of job he would be able to do for us. Anything else which requires discussion comes later.

It was the same with Mo today. About five minutes after my first question to Walter about Mo the religious side of the signing was discussed. That took about an hour because it was a complicated matter and it was something we knew would create special problems for the club and for ourselves. But we agreed that a Catholic had to be signed at some stage and that we wanted to do it. It was never going to be some token signing – it was only going to happen IF the player was someone we wanted. Mo fitted that description.

I thought about the matter some more at home and then I telephoned the chairman, David Murray, and put the whole thing to him. He took it on board and suggested that we meet in the morning. Tomorrow promises to be an eventful day in the history of the club and certainly the most eventful in the three years I have been here at Ibrox.

4 July 1989

We met today at Ibrox and discussed the situation regarding Mo Johnston. We went into every aspect. Everyone accepted that he was a world-class striker. Everyone accepted that since going to France his image had improved off the field, as well as his ability on it. And everyone agreed that the club had maintained for many years that there would be a Catholic signing. I was asked the question myself when I took over as manager and I said that religion would never be a barrier for me if I wanted a player. In my first season I tried to buy Ray Houghton from Oxford but the player, born in Glasgow though he plays for the Republic of Ireland, did not fancy making the move. He ended up at Liverpool and his class has been underlined there just as it was when he played for Ireland in the European Championships last summer. I would have torn down the barrier then but the player would not sign. We have to find out if Mo will.

I talked to his agent after the meeting and he is ready to set up a meeting immediately. It will mean flying to France and I am ready to go there. Mo is ready to talk to us but the whole thing has to be kept very quiet at this stage. We don't want to risk anything going wrong – as it did for Celtic. We just want to speak to the player, find out how he reacts to the whole idea of joining us and then take it from there. If he is the same as Ray Houghton then there is little point in trying to buy him from the French club. If he is willing to risk the obvious hostility he will face in Glasgow then we can go for it.

All of us feel this move would finish the problems of discrimination once and for all. No one will be able to point the finger at the club any longer. I want to do it. So does the chairman and so does every other member of the club. It is a risk but it is one we are prepared to take. All of us. What we have to discover is whether Mo will take the risk with us.

7 July 1989

I flew to Paris this morning with our chief executive Alan Montgomery to meet Mo Johnston and his agent. We arranged to meet them at Orly Airport where the flights from Nantes arrive. It was essential that no one would find out about the journey in case they were able to put two and two together. We kept it as quiet as possible and yet, even allowing that we have done all of this under as much strict secrecy as possible, rumours are sweeping Glasgow that we are going to sign the player.

There is no way we want this leaked. Everything has to be settled before the public get the news. It is going to be controversial and it is going to cause a great deal of comment and we want to be prepared for that.

We left the airport and went to a little coffee shop not too far away. It was there that we had the discussions on the deal which is going to rock Scottish football. There we were, the four of us, sitting in this tiny French café with a little old Frenchwoman serving us coffees at around ten o'clock in the morning. She must have been wondering what on earth we were up to. If only she'd known that she was sitting in on a one-and-a-half million pound transfer deal. I know that the fans like to think that all these deals are finalised in luxury hotels or top restaurants with champagne being served to everyone. That's far from the truth. When you are determined to keep a low profile then you talk terms wherever you can! In this case it was that little café near Orly Airport. You know, it seemed so important today and yet I doubt if I would ever be able to find it again. A momentous meeting place and I can't remember where it is. That is really crazy.

But it has all been worthwhile. Mo has agreed to join us immediately. As far as the football side of the deal is concerned he has no doubts whatsoever. He jumped at the chance of coming aboard. It was after that he raised the question of the religious problems which will affect his life. I gave him some time to think that over – like a minute-and-a-half – and that was it. No, seriously, he had given it some thought before the meeting and he went into various aspects of it with us. We tried to satisfy him as best we could because none of us know how the signing will be accepted. It is a step into the unknown for every one of us.

We are no different from Mo as far as that is concerned. But we do have a responsibility to any player signing for us and that is to help him find a home where he will have some kind of privacy and a reasonable home life. We have promised to help Mo with this. But that is standard procedure for any player coming to join us. Or a player who is going to any big club, I suppose.

I was impressed with Mo's willingness to join us. He wants to be a part of what we are trying to achieve at Ibrox. He wanted to play back home, he wanted to be with a BIG club and he wanted to play in the European Cup as well as the World Cup. All of these, of course, were on offer to him. Like ourselves when we first thought of the signing, the footballing part was not a problem. The rest – well, we have to try to make it all as easy as possible for him and allow him to concentrate on his game.

It's funny to think of it. Here we are, the main people in the deal, and on my side all I want to think about is how good a player Mo is and how much he will improve Rangers as a team. And on his side all he wants is to play with a top club. The other aspects of the deal don't concern us. Nor should they. Unhappily they will take precedence when the news breaks. There will be more words written about the religious question than there will be about Mo's ability. That surely cannot be right?

We took a taxi back to Orly with the player and his agent, shook hands once again on the deal in the cab and left them to tidy up their affairs with Nantes. Alan and I went on in the cab to Charles De Gaulle Airport for our return flight to Glasgow. I felt a sense of relief on that journey home and, I suppose, too, a few pangs of worry over what might lie ahead for all of us when we make the announcement of the signing. But I am clear in my own mind that what I have done here is the very best for Rangers Football Club. That is what I have tried to do ever since I arrived as manager. I genuinely believe I have done it all along and I still feel that over this signing. He is a world-class striker and that should count for more than what school he went to or what church he goes to now. I think the club will benefit from this. We will have broken down a barrier which was not of our making and which has been, at times, an embarrassment to everyone at Ibrox. It was essential that it should be done and I am glad that with the backing of David Murray I have been the man to do it.

8 July 1989

So far, so good. We arrived back without being seen. And, while the rumours continue to grow, no one is giving them any credence. It is the way we want it and it is the way that we have to handle this transfer. For all the reasons I have spelled out already this is a delicate negotiation. We cannot afford to see it go sour on us.

I have spoken to the chairman and he is delighted that we seem to have pulled off another major signing coup. He is equally delighted that we have kept everything under wraps. He is as aware as all of us are that the decision to sign a Catholic player will not be greeted well by some of our support. We have to prepare ourselves for that – and we know that it will be

Mo Johnston at Ibrox to sign along with his new manager Graeme Souness.

exacerbated by the fact that the player is an ex-Celtic player and one who was going to sign for them again earlier this summer.

This adds its own little bit of drama to the whole thing. Again, though, that has never been a concern of mine. I don't see why it should be. If we manage to sign a player ahead of, say, Manchester United, Spurs or Liverpool we are praised for doing so. We found that out when we signed Terry Butcher and Spurs wanted him and then a few weeks ago we were being praised again for signing Trevor Steven when Manchester United were poised to get him. We also signed Ian Ferguson – a player that my mate Kenny Dalglish had wanted. We kept him in Scottish soccer where people could see his talents grow. Now we have signed Scotland's centre-forward and it should not matter which team he played for before or who tried to sign him. The bottom line is that he will be our player next week and, again, people will have the chance to watch him week in and week out – not just when Scotland have a World Cup game at Hampden. I just hope that people recognise what we are doing here – not only ending discrimination at the club but also bringing a class player back home to play in the Premier League. Essentially that is what this deal is about.

10 July 1989

The balloon went up this morning. The story that we are going to sign Mo Johnston was blasted across the front and back pages of the *Sun*. There were other pages inside the paper, too. We thought that all our security ploys had worked. Now, at the very end, the story has been used before our announcement.

Our press conference was called for ten o'clock this morning and even though the *Sun*'s story had been seen by everyone in the media there were still doubts, I think, whether it was the Johnston signing we were ready to announce. But when we brought him through to meet the press no doubts remained. The die had been cast. The whole world of football knew that the promise I made when I joined Rangers was being kept. I said then that I did not believe in any form of religious discrimination and that I would sign any player of any persuasion if it meant

*The moment which stunned Scottish soccer – Mo Johnston walks
into the famous Blue Room at Ibrox to meet the media. Looking
on are owner David Murray and chief executive Alan
Montgomery as manager Graeme Souness leads Johnston in.*

strengthening the team. We had tried before and we had failed. Now it has happened. Now it is reality.

History was made in the Blue Room at Ibrox this morning and for all the people who don't agree with the signing there are thousands more who do. I am not arrogant enough to think that only my views should prevail, that only I can be right – though some people will try to say that is exactly how I am. All I can say to the supporters who disagree is that they are entitled to their views, but that my job is to do all that I can for this club in my bid to make it one of the best teams in Europe. That is all that concerns me and it is all that I am going to allow to concern me. I am utterly single-minded about this. I want Rangers to be the best and if I fall out with people while I aim for that, then that is the way it has to be. They can have their opinions – but I will have mine. And as long as I am the manager then my opinions will be the ones that count most of all.

I would like to think, too, that maybe this decision of mine will make it easier in the future for whoever else becomes manager of the club. They won't have to face up to the particular problem of religious discrimination which bedevilled my first three years at Ibrox. That is now a thing of the past. Hopefully it will soon be forgotten.

And if by this move we have helped ease the tensions in the west of Scotland, then that is even better. I am not going to pretend that was our intention. Football was the first issue – and whether Mo would make us better or not. The attendant issues were considered and we all hope that eventually some good and maybe a greater understanding will follow as well. But we can only take one step at a time and we know that. Everyone is waiting to see if this works out. I remain convinced that it will.

11 July 1989

We appear to have won over most of the support – certainly the signing has been welcomed in many areas of life in Scotland. Some of the newspapers have been whole-hearted in their support. Others – and I find this surprising – have been a little grudging. I don't know why anyone should do other than praise what we have done here. For years Rangers have been pilloried for what the majority of people saw as discrimination against one section of the population. Now we have shown that this unwritten policy at Ibrox is over. It's finished. Done with. Yet, still, there seem to be pockets of opinion who will not give us due credit no matter what we do.

It doesn't bother me too much any longer. It seems to be part of the situation which we have inherited at the club. Too many people are ready to snipe at Rangers Football Club whether they have cause to do so or not. Now we have taken away one area where we could be constantly criticised and we have done it for the best of motives. I know I have written this already, but I cannot say it often enough. We bought Mo Johnston because he is a top player. We bought him to make Rangers a better team. We bought him because we want to have the very best players available here at Ibrox.

It would not have been right for us to sign anyone simply to emphasise that there is no discrimination. I think that would have been wrong. The first priority at this club as long as I am manager will be the player's ability. That has to come first. To do anything else would not be right. No other club would sign players – or be expected to sign players – on any other basis. We should not be treated differently. Sure, the signing is a milestone, but that was a secondary consideration and it was a consideration only because of what had happened here in the years before David Murray and myself arrived on the scene. Religion – any religion – will never be the pre-eminent motive behind any signing I make. It never could be. If I had turned away from signing Mo Johnston because he was a Catholic then my judgment would have been warped. It would not have been the right thing to do and it would have been hypocrisy of the worst kind on my part. I married a Catholic after all.

It would be wrong to say that everyone is happy. We have had suggestions that season tickets will be returned, that others will be torn up. A couple of fans have burned their scarves outside the stadium. They are, I suppose, entitled to make these gestures. But no matter what they do they will not change the minds of any of the people at the club who were involved in the decision

17

A picture taken a few weeks earlier shows Mo and girlfriend Karen when he seemed poised to join the OTHER team in Glasgow.

to make this signing. What we want now is for the supporters who have backed us all the way in the past three years to give us their backing once more. They saw the English players come north and maybe a few of them wondered what was happening to the club. Then they saw the quality players who arrived. They saw the successes the club achieved and they welcomed what had happened.

I can't tell you how many of the supporters have told me that this is the kind of Rangers they have wanted, a team living up to the reputation of greatness that has always hung around Ibrox. I genuinely believe that a whole lot of people wanted to see the club broaden its horizons and become BIG in the European sense. I did not see that we could do that only with Scottish players – especially in the state the club was when I took over. I had to get the top players who were available and in Scotland few were available to us. No one wants to sell to Rangers. Other clubs don't want to let us have their players and so we had to look elsewhere.

Anyhow, the fans came with us. They have been superb and if anyone outside ourselves and our support doubts that they need only look at the attendances we have had over the past few years. We have given the fans what they wanted most – SUCCESS. That is still what we want them to have and I'm sure the majority will recognise that fact. We can only hope that the criticisms are isolated and that the 40,000 or so people who clamour to get in to the games week after week will form the majority and will welcome Mo Johnston.

We are not underestimating the problems he faces and we face along with him. Predictably there have been threats against him and so he has decided to live away from the west of Scotland. Mo may be a little worried himself but he knows that we are doing everything possible for him. The way he is accepted by the players will help. We flew to Tuscany today and he was welcomed by everyone. I wish the fans who have protested could have seen that. These players know that we have signed a class act. That is all that matters to them. And, really, it's all that should matter to anyone!

22 July 1989

Mo played his first game today – behind closed doors at Broomfield. Despite speculation that there would be demonstrations by angry fans nothing happened at the Airdrie ground. I think there were more pressmen there than fans. Now that the furore has started to die down we seem to be getting the support from the fans that we hoped for. The complaints have lessened and there have been few attempts to send season tickets back. Indeed, there is still a huge waiting list for these tickets. The few which are returned will be snapped up. Talk of boycotts seems to be so much rubbish.

On the football side Mo looked sharp in the game and picked up three goals. Not a bad start ... but he will play there again next Saturday in a Testimonial Match for two of the Airdrie players and that will be in front of a sell-out crowd. It will be a bigger test for him. And it will be a test for all of us over the whole affair. That will be the first time that the fans, *en masse*, will have a chance to shout the odds if that's what they want to do. Or they can simply welcome him the way they have welcomed all the other players over the past three seasons.

29 July 1989

No sign of any Broomfield boycott, I'm glad to say. The fans turned out and we had the bulk of the support in the sell-out crowd. It gave the two Airdrie lads a nice little boost and for us it was a game we needed pre-season. Mo played. He did not score but he looked good. And the fans took to him. They applauded him when he went on to the field for a warm up beforehand. They applauded him when he came on for the game itself, and there were roars of encouragement all the way through.

It was what we had hoped for – maybe even better than we had hoped for. I could not have been any happier with the way they accepted him and I told the press that afterwards. I know that Mo did the same. Sure, he was nervous, especially as it was his first game in public since joining us. But apart from some jibes from the Airdrie fans – and he is well used to the opposition

Another look at the duo which shocked soccer – Mo Johnston and Souness.

jeering him – it all turned out right. It was a concern for us beforehand and I'd like to mention here the few hundred fans who were outside Ibrox when the team bus left there. They cheered the players as they left the stadium and Mo was cheered the same as the others. That eased the tension before we even got to Broomfield.

The support overall was more than we had looked for. It showed that the majority of the fans are with us. All we want is that to continue through the season. You know, I think we all thought there would be some isolated jeers from some of the fans who did not like the signing. They did not make themselves heard here – and that is to their credit as well as to the credit of all the Rangers' supporters.

Mind you, we still have one hurdle to face. That will come at the annual meeting of the club, which is to be held at Ibrox next week. Perhaps there will be opposition voiced then. The annual meeting has the reputation of being troublesome at times when things are going wrong or when anything happens to upset the people with shares in the club. We will have to wait and see.

3 August 1989

The annual meeting was held at Ibrox and there were almost 2,000 people there. After the board were congratulated on signing Mo Johnston there were others who shouted against the move. The chairman explained why the transfer had taken place and I spoke too. Obviously there were people who did not like what we had done and they took their chance to say so. But, equally, we were able to carry the bulk of the meeting with us. There were isolated pockets of criticism in the crowd. Yet, again, the demonstrations against the signing which had been predicted in some quarters did not come.

Walking along the street back to the front door of Ibrox after the meeting, people stopped to say they were behind me in all that was happening at Ibrox. That was gratifying. I honestly think we have got it right. Maybe it was the right time for the change. Maybe the fans were readier to accept it than they might have been ten years earlier. I don't know. I think about the move constantly and I have worried over it too. Now, after two games where Mo has had no problems and after this meeting where the board were up there on stage for any shareholder to have a go at we have come through relatively unscathed. Again it was better than any of the predictions had suggested and better than I expected.

New team-mates – Terry Butcher with former Celtic star Mo Johnston who joined up at Ibrox in the summer.

The Scotland and Rangers' front men – Ally McCoist and his new Ibrox mate Mo Johnston.

One time opponents, now team-mates in a training game in Tuscany soon after Mo Johnston's controversial transfer to Rangers. Here Mo is facing up to John Brown with Gary Stevens lying in wait.

Flat out! Mo Johnston after an early training session with Rangers in Italy.

2

Secrets of a Six Million Pound Takeover!

Perhaps, eventually, the Mo Johnston signing was to usurp the earlier club takeover as the major news story of another season of headlines for Rangers. Yet it was just as significant a step for the club. Here was manager Graeme Souness, tipped by so many people to move on after a spell in charge at Ibrox, putting up a massive amount of his own personal cash to take a stake in the club along with his close friend David Murray.

The Edinburgh-based millionaire supplied the bulk of the cash – almost six million pounds. But Souness put in more than half a million to underline again his commitment to Rangers. The takeover announcement came out of the blue. No one suspected. No one outside the principals knew what was happening. Secret meetings were set up between Murray and Lawrence Marlborough. Talks between Murray and Souness took place over a period of months as it became clear that the club could be up for grabs.

Souness was clearly determined that if and when it was sold he should become involved. He did so – and anyone who ever doubted just how much he feels for Rangers was forced into a re-think. The man who captained Liverpool to so much success wants to have the same success – or even more – as a manager.

He wants to see Rangers as one of the great clubs of Europe. He wants them to be talked about in the same breath as AC Milan or Juventus or Real Madrid or Bayern Munich. He sees no reason why that should not happen under the new owner. He believes that David Murray will make them the BEST – and he is there to help him do that.

The inside story of the deal is told here, from the first whispered suggestions to the full blown purchase of the club and the plans for the future.

5 July 1988

Training starts and I'm beginning to wonder what the season will hold for us. After winning the title in my first season last year's happenings were often traumatic. Not just from my own point of view but from the points of view of everyone connected with the club. The title lost. Players in court. A bad, bad season by any standards.

It has made me wonder just how everyone else is feeling about the various events. I found it difficult and I know the players did too. But I am also concerned about what is happening behind the scenes. I have a feeling that the chairman has lost some of his enthusiasm. I would never have believed that possible. During my first season David Holmes was a tower of strength to myself and Walter Smith – maybe now he has had enough. He took a buffeting on all sides last season. Perhaps that explains why he is not quite as bouncy as he was before.

Funnily enough I was talking to David Murray and he has asked me to let him know if the club is ever on the market. Who knows? Perhaps that will happen – even though it is something I would never have dreamed possible when I came here first of all. But things change and if seven days is a long time in politics then it is often even longer in this game! It is something to think about when we go off to Italy and the training game there next week.

The bright news is that Terry Butcher started training with the rest of the lads today. He looks good and while we missed him so badly last season I am convinced that the summer of rest will have helped his recovery. It was a blow to him to miss the European Championships but the rest was essential. Incidentally, it was a blow to England too. I reckon they missed the big fellow as much as we did during the season!

30 September 1988

Dinner with David Murray. The usual Friday night meeting and at our usual Italian restaurant in Edinburgh. The feeling is still there that Rangers may be ready to go for a change in ownership and I still think that David Murray would be the man for it. He was interested in buying Ayr United and that fell through for him. It was their mistake, I think, because he has a lot to offer the game. I still have the feeling that he could be the man for Rangers if Lawrence Marlborough ever decides that he wants to get out. And I still have a hunch that this will happen.

Even though we have started the season so well and some of the problems we had last season have been shown to be only temporary hiccups in what we are trying to build and trying to achieve here, there is still less of that first season euphoria around. I know that won't be around all the time but the feelings still persist that with the Lawrence Group concentrating so much on fresh developments in the States, a buyer for Rangers would not be out of the ball park as far as they are concerned.

Maybe I am wrong. Maybe it is in my mind because I am friendly with David and I have said to him already that if he wants into football then it should be at the top. He has done so well in basketball but that has surely started to pall a little for him. Football is the BIG game here in Scotland and if he wants in then it should not be at the Ayr United level, and maybe it should not be for the sentimental reasons which led him towards Ayr in the first place. Ayr was where he grew up, there were family connections and he supported the club as a boy. But is that enough? After all, he has also had a soft spot for Rangers for a large part of his life and it would make better sense to come in at our level rather than try to take a club up from the lower divisions. That could be heartbreaking. OK, so can running a club as big as this one but the rewards when they come are so much greater. And they are attainable! I told David that again tonight and he smiled. He said as he has said before that if there was movement then I should keep him in touch with the situation.

I have been friendly with David almost since the day and hour I arrived back in Scotland. I had known about him, of course, and heard about him. And I knew about the basketball involvement which he had and which he had built up so well. I met him at his hotel – he had the Norton House then – when the basketball player Alton Bird introduced us. It has been a good friendship – but people say friends should not go into business together. I hope that is not right. This could be a starter and I think it would be good for the club, good for David and good for the supporters. It could be a very important move all round.

The throwaway line I gave over dinner months ago about him buying Rangers may not have been far off the mark. He is the kind of man who should be with a top club. And, as far as I am concerned, no club in Britain is bigger than Rangers. If he deserves the best, then he should get himself involved with Rangers. And if the club deserves the best – and I happen to think they do – then David Murray could be the man. He wants success in anything he becomes involved in. That is a trait I recognise. And respect. So do Rangers' fans!

The problem is that there are no obvious signs from Ibrox yet that they would be willing to listen to any takeover bid. My personal hunches could be wrong. I could be looking at things, adding them up and landing myself with all the wrong answers. Soon I will have to make a move and then see how positively David reacts. It is the only way.

11 October 1988

The time has come. I have spoken to the chairman David Holmes

A sight which Rangers' fans probably won't be able to enjoy again – manager Graeme Souness in on-field action. Souness says that is now a thing of the past.

and I have told him that David Murray may be interested in buying the club. My hunches seem to have been right – the idea is taken on board. We could be in business. David is poised, ready to move whenever he gets the green light.

I have told David that I am ready to be part of the package he prepares. Owning a part of the club excites me. And if my own money is in then it should stop the knockers telling people that I am only at Ibrox until something bigger turns up. How could you get any bigger club? It beats me but they still persist in believing that I am only along for a joy ride. They hit the players with that same insult last season. According to the critics they were just a bunch of mercenaries – and that is probably how they want to see me too. I reckon we will all prove them wrong.

The amazing thing is that two-and-a-bit years ago I was happily playing away in the Italian First Division, coasting towards a retirement from the game. Now, here I am in Scotland, back home and working out how we can buy the biggest club in the country. The game has lots of twists, lots of very strange moves, and lots of surprises. But this one is the biggest I have ever been involved in. Coming back home to be the manager of Rangers caused a bit of a sensation. I wonder how this is going to go down when the media find out?

The essential thing, though, is not to allow a whisper to leak. This cannot be allowed to be talked about until the deal has been done. So many things can go wrong and football is such a gossip factory. Everyone involved has to be sworn to secrecy. There can be no other way. If any hint appears anywhere other potential buyers could come in and if that happens then it would be impossible, perhaps, for me to carry on.

I believe that David Murray offers the right future and the proper ambition for this club. He BELIEVES in Rangers as a force in British and European football. He recognises that the borders are coming down and that any club with real ambition has to be ready to face the challenge from the continent when that happens. We have to be ready for that and too many people in the game don't seem to be able to grasp the idea. At Ibrox we have always seen the direction the game is taking – and David can see it for himself. The next few weeks of negotiation and secret talks are going to be exciting. I want them to work out right. For Rangers' sake as well as for my own and David Murray's.

21 October 1988

The wheels are now in motion. David has had a meeting with Lawrence Marlborough and the chairman and the takeover idea is a goer. I met David for our usual Friday meal tonight and it is funny how things have changed. Normally we are pretty outgoing in this restaurant because we like it there, we are comfortable there and we know the people. Now, of course, secrecy is everything. When the waiters come to the table we are talking in whispers. We don't want to allow the slightest word to give anyone a clue. We have taken to talking of the deal only when we are on our own and when we are together – the phone is OUT. The waiters in the restaurant must have seen a change. David is normally so flamboyant and yet here we are – conspirators. And behaving that way. I hope that does not give anyone an inkling of what is happening. Surely not? It has been kept so secure from all angles. Yet we still worry.

I sometimes feel that you cannot keep anything secret in football. Jusk ask any manager who has been involved in a major transfer. There always seems to be some leak. This time, though, we want to be leak-proof. The fact that the Skol Cup final is looming, plus games in Europe, keeps the media attention focused on the playing side. Thank God for that! Let's hope that this can be tied up soon.

I am happy that I read the script properly. When David and Lawrence Marlborough met at David's Edinburgh HQ everything seemed right and I want it to stay that way. I think that we all do. This is one of the most important steps I have ever taken in my life. It is not one which I have taken lightly. This club has come to mean more and more to me. I learn something about it almost every day of my life. Something which illustrates that the club is special. I knew a bit about that before I came. I have learned more, much more, since... .

20 November 1988

We dropped another point yesterday but with the injuries we have been suffering that did not surprise me too much. It is sad, though, that we should hit a little bit of a rocky spell when so much is happening behind the scenes. Still no one knows. Still the charmed circle has kept everything under wraps – even though the circle, through necessity, has had to expand from the original handful.

Today the most important meeting so far was held and now everything is in place. The price has been agreed between Lawrence Marlborough and David Murray. The meetings which have taken place so far have obviously convinced Lawrence that the club is going into good hands. I have always felt that and I said so when the takeover was first mooted. I hope that Lawrence and the chairman realised that I would not want the club to fall into the hands of someone who would not have its best interests at heart. The buyer had to be acceptable, he had to be the kind of man who would carry on the job which was started by Lawrence Marlborough and David Holmes. The job they asked me to do and Walter Smith to do alongside me. The job of taking Rangers back to the top where they belong. We are not there yet. We are making progress and we are on the road we want to be on, but the job is not anything like over. It had to be a man who would see that through and I know that David Murray is that kind of man.

Anyhow I have been involved in some of the meetings and everything has been thrashed out. Maybe a few fine details have to be sorted out but the deal is ON! The legal men have to draw up all the papers but hopefully this will be concluded this week and the worry over leaks will be over. The strain has been tremendous. Yet somehow despite the glare of publicity which is focused on Ibrox for 24 hours a day, seven days a week nothing has got out.

Maybe I have got David into something so big that he does not quite realise it – but I know he will enjoy it. I have told him how big Rangers arè and I have told his wife, too, that this will start to take over their lives. You don't get much of a chance to walk

Another title has been won and Graeme Souness enjoys himself at Ibrox.

away from the limelight when Rangers are involved. Anything you do is news. You learn to live with that. David says it won't affect him – but it will. We will wait and see how that one goes. But I have seen the picture... .

This club becomes an all-consuming passion for anyone who gets involved. You cannot help yourself. I used to think that Liverpool was mad about its football – it doesn't reach the same passion which is produced by the people who follow, follow Rangers. I have seen it all for myself and David is going to learn about it from the inside. He will be a part of the club and I know he will be an active part because he is a 'hands-on' kind of guy. He buys something, be it another business or a football club, and he wants to know what is going on there. He won't be making this kind of major investment to sit back and relax. He will get himself involved and then he will learn what we have all learned – that Rangers takes over your very life.

Anyhow, most important of all is that the next meeting – and that is the BIG one – will be held this week. It looks as if it will be on Tuesday. Then everything will be signed. The Is will be dotted and the Ts will be crossed and the club will change hands. I know that this must be an emotional moment for Lawrence Marlborough whose grandfather was chairman and was the man who did so much to build the club into its present position. Losing a family tie cannot be easy for anyone, especially as the club does take such a hold on your emotions and your life.

But this is an emotional time for me too. I am on the verge of owning a major part – or a relatively major part – in the biggest club in Britain. Not only that, but a casual remark made to a friend so many months ago has now flowered into a huge multi-million pounds takeover. It is an awesome responsibility and, yet, I am enjoying a lot of this. And I am going to enjoy it even more when we can make the formal announcement. The whole deal excites me. The future always did look bright with this club – now I see it as even brighter. I doubt if David Murray's ambitions know any limits. We are probably well matched in that way. I feel the same and I know that the players I have brought here feel the same. What we have achieved so far may only be the beginning. Watch this space... .

22 November 1988

The final meeting is tonight and still the security remains tight enough to please us all. The meeting is at Ibrox in the boardroom and then the various documents will be signed. Everything has been agreed in principle. Everything has been worked out. The price is going to be six million pounds and, as well as that, the buyers of the club, David Murray and yours truly, will inherit the overdraft which the club has. That is running at several million pounds as well, but I still see this deal as a bargain – or, at the very least, a really good buy. David feels the same.

The potential at Ibrox is limitless. I have always told David that and I knew that he was listening to all that I did tell him. But now he has had a close look at things along with his advisers and I think he has realised what I have realised in my years here – Rangers are the biggest club in Britain. And we have to stand alongside the European giants. The facilities here are magnificent. The stadium fulfils all that the UEFA and FIFA planners will require in the future. The launch pad is in place. The only question mark I can see is just how far we can take the club in the future.

What we don't need now are hitches. Things have been kept so carefully under wraps, and the talks have progressed so well, that we do not want any late hold ups in the deal going through. I don't think that will happen somehow. The relationship between the Lawrence Group people and ourselves has been marvellous. I would imagine the meeting tonight being a simple formality – and then we can make the announcement!

23 November 1988

I am looking at what I wrote yesterday before the meeting. I should not have been so hopeful, though it did turn out OK in the end. But the agreement was signed just three minutes before the stroke of midnight, which had become something of a legal deadline. To add to the problems which surfaced in the huge amount of paper work involved, there was a late enquiry for the club. Just when everything seemed sewn up, Robert Maxwell phoned one of the merchant bankers who was involved in the setting up of the deal to express interest.

David wanted the deal clinched immediately when he heard of this late intervention. But there were some points which had to be clarified, details to be emphasised – in essence the lawyers had to perform some fine tuning in the wording of the documents. The problem was that the documents were dated for 22 November and as midnight approached all of us suddenly realised that they would have to be drawn up again if they were not signed before the day ended. Six minutes to midnight and another minor alteration was made. Five minutes to go and it was examined by the principals and agreed. Three minutes before deadline and the papers were signed. Any hopes that Robert Maxwell may have had of moving in to add Glasgow Rangers to the clubs he already controlled in England had vanished.

This morning the club announced a press conference and everyone came to Ibrox in the afternoon. Earlier though, I spoke to two newspapermen whom I could trust and told them what was happening. They did not believe me at first, especially when I said that I had bought part of the club. They had had no idea. Security sometimes does work, even in football!

By the afternoon, of course, the word has spread and the newspapers and the cameras are ready. David is going to get his first taste of the publicity which will shortly surround his every move and his every statement. The conference goes well. Lawrence Marlborough tells everyone how big a wrench it has been for him – but living in the States has made his overseeing of the club a long distance one. He adds: ''I am delighted that the new custodian is such a personable and dynamic young man, that he is Scottish-based and that he is a Rangers' supporter.''

Then David stepped forward to say his piece with a reference to the Maxwell enquiry for the club. He said simply: ''I am delighted that this takeover means that a Scottish institution remains in Scottish hands. We intend to provide a strong base for the continuing development of the club and its business aspects. I see Rangers as the leading club in Scotland and I believe it will become a major force in the game in Europe. We want to take Rangers forward into a new era of achievement.''

It was simple. It was straightforward and it reflected the way the whole business had been handled. Only these late hiccups had caused any of us any worries at all. And they vanished in time for the documents to be properly signed. So now I am a director of the club. As well as a player. And the manager. When I am asked how I feel I have to admit that two-and-a-half years ago when I took a telephone call in Genoa asking me if I would be interested in being player-manager of Rangers I never envisaged anything like this. The incredible thing is that from the time I spoke to David Murray seriously about it and then spoke to the chairman David Holmes, the whole takeover has been handled inside a six-week spell. Buying a player can sometimes take longer! In fact, I have had to wait longer than that for one or two of the men I have signed for Rangers.

It all seems a little bit incredible now. All those talks with David in an Italian restaurant in Edinburgh have led to this. He is a man I admire and a man I believe I will work well with. We want the same success for Rangers. At home. And in Europe. It would be nice to be able to hand him the title at the end of April to celebrate his first season in charge. We will have to go for that because, knowing him, he will want it.

24 November 1988

David has had his first taste of the media interest in the club. He had all the television coverage last night. But today he is on the front page of every newspaper in Scotland.

People still seem to find it hard to understand why I have taken a personal stake in the club. But I know why. I just have to look out at my garden and remember the years I spent travelling around the country and eventually the continent, playing football. From the time I left home I was never at rest. As a kid I was at Spurs and living down there in London. Then, not too much more than a kid, I was in the Middlesbrough side playing there. Next it was on to Liverpool and then to Genoa after I joined Sampdoria. Then I came here as manager, arriving at a club whose potential is enormous. I felt then and I feel now that if I can make this work for Rangers then I will never want to go anywhere else.

In a business sense I think it is a good deal for me. I also think it is good for David and I believe that my own involvement helped sway him towards the takeover. I mentioned earlier in this diary that old saying that you should not go into partnership with a friend. Maybe that will be proved right in the future – but I hope not. And I don't think so. We are on the same wavelength and that wavelength is this club Rangers. That will become even more so once David becomes really involved and I know he will do that. Exciting times are ahead for all of us... .

25 November 1988

The dust has started to settle and David and I meet in Raffaelli's as usual. For dinner. As usual. But things have changed. As well as friends we are now also partners with aims we want to achieve together.

Tomorrow we face Aberdeen at Ibrox. They are still unbeaten in the Premier League and are now snapping at our heels. As well as being a nice little present for the new owner, a victory would be vitally important to us. Yet we are still without Chris Woods whose viral infection is now causing us a bit of real concern. And Ally McCoist is out as well. He has been missing for a few games. Going in against Aberdeen with these problems, added to the Ian Durrant tragedy, doesn't make life easy.

Today I spoke to Kenny Dalglish and he agreed to give me Kevin MacDonald on loan. He will be in our plans for the Aberdeen game even though he has been out of the first-team plans at Liverpool. He has to be – we are running short of players because of the injury toll. I tell David all about this and as we talk he starts off by saying that it would be good to get a win tomorrow. I agree. Later he says how much we need to win. Again I agree. By the end of the meal he is telling me that we had better win tomorrow. There is no answer to that – except a welcoming win tomorrow afternoon.

26 November 1988

The new owner takes his seat in the Ibrox directors' box for the first time. The crowd roar their welcome. If he had harboured any worries about the reaction from the support they must surely have disappeared immediately. He gets the treatment. The full Rangers' welcome from more than 40,000 fans.

Ally McCoist reads about the new deal he signed – a long-term one which will keep him at Ibrox for years to come.

We win 1-0 from a goal scored by Richard Gough just a couple of minutes before half-time. Kevin MacDonald plays for a spell as substitute and does OK. But the need to sign him has underlined again to me how much of a problem we have when injuries hit the first-team squad. There is still work to be done over strengthening the player pool. Walter Smith and myself have known that but it has to be apparent to everyone now.

Of course we are not just missing three players, we are missing three INTERNATIONAL players. That is a handicap most clubs would not be able to overcome. Today we have done so and the two points are important. They push us four points beyond Aberdeen and the crowd who watch us open up that gap is a massive 42,239 – the biggest in Britain. And not for the first time. No doubt David has noted that too!

I think he will know the tension which can grip you now. I am not suggesting that he did not accept that people involved with the club felt the tension – but experiencing it yourself brings it all home to you.

The Premier League situation looks good just now, even though we faltered a little after that tremendous start. But there is a long, long way to go and a lot more points to be won and lost before we can even think too seriously about it. It has become a cliché, I know, but the only way to approach a long, drawn-out competition is by taking each game on its own. Win the next one and you are two points closer. Keep going on like that and eventually you will be champions. There is no other way to do it. Start looking too far ahead about what might happen here, there and everywhere and you will slip up. It's not about what other clubs can do for you, it's all about what you can do for yourself. No one wins titles for you.

20 January 1989

Another Friday meeting with David Murray. There is a change in David now. More and more he is becoming steeped in the club and what we want to do. And he is not afraid to tell me what he wants – friend or not. That is the way it should be. It has to be that kind of relationship because I don't reckon it would work any other way. I may be a director and I may be the second-largest shareholder – but I am also still the manager and I remain answerable to the board of Rangers Football Club as far as the on-field results are concerned. I still know that I can be sacked. If the results don't come then I would be off. It is as simple as that and I would not have it any other way because no other way would it all work.

I knew when I came here that I had to make the club successful. David Holmes and Lawrence Marlborough spelled that out to Walter and myself when we were appointed. We knew then that if we flopped we would be sacked. We were told that – right up front! Again that is the way it should be. Better that than directors giving you the big vote of confidence while they are getting someone else to take your job. Anyone who is in this game as a manager knows that he is only secure in his job IF he wins. When the losing starts then you are in trouble. And because I have a few shares in the club that won't make me exempt. I'll be axed just as anyone else would be. Becoming a director doesn't grant you immunity.

Sometimes I think about it all and it is still difficult for it to sink in. I pinch myself every now and again. But there have been no basic changes to my job. It is still a case of getting the best team on the field – injuries permitting. And when it comes to talking transfers I speak to David directly and tell him what I might need. To some extent I am putting our friendship under strain but we both know that.

I can remember saying to David: "Do you know what you are doing here. Do you know exactly what you are taking on?" He told me he did and my answer to that was to tell him that the club would take over his life. He pooh-poohed that. He pointed out how many other businesses he had to handle and how much time he had to give them. But I think if he sat down now to talk about Rangers he would admit that it takes a far bigger chunk out of his life than he ever imagined it would. I found that. Walter Smith found that. David Holmes found that.

And, talking personally, I love every minute of it. I can hardly wait to get along that M8 every morning and get into Ibrox and get started on the day. Walter is the same and that is the way it grips you. I'm glad I warned David because there is no escape. Not that any of us wants one.

24 February 1989

We have St Mirren tomorrow. I talk to David Murray about Mel Sterland. The deal might have gone through by now but there has been a delay because of a managerial change which has taken place at Sheffield Wednesday. Peter Eustace has gone while Ron Atkinson has come in to take his job. I impress on David the need to sign the player. He is a good all-round professional. He has played in a handful of positions for Sheffield Wednesday, including striker! But we need him for cover. We don't want to have come this far in the race for the Premier League and then find ourselves short of players if someone is suspended.

The discipline amongst the players has been superb this season. I set out our stall before the year began because I did not want to face yet another round of criticism about the number of players who were in trouble. I promised publicly that we would clean up our act – and we have done that. We are sitting close to the top of the B and Q Fair Play League which is organised by the Scottish League and that pleases me almost as much as being at the top of the Premier Division. But, come the end of the season, no matter how hard players try to stay out of trouble, bookings have occurred and penalty points have mounted. Big Terry is close to suspension and while he wants to avoid it and will try to avoid it, a suspension could come his way and leave us without an important part of our defence. We struggled through without key players because of injury and we don't want to have to limp towards the title if that can be avoided. Mel Sterland can give us cover and I have told David this. He agrees that we should pursue our bid for the player.

I see a change in David now. He is now totally caught up in things. He is completely a part of the cause – the Rangers' cause. He is a very intelligent man, a very rational man but where everything was black and white before, now everything is blue! All I can say is that I did tell him. It happened to me after I had been at Ibrox a little while and I have been in professional football all my life. That includes the passion I experienced on Merseyside and the passion in Italy. But I had my eyes opened here and it took a hold on me just as it has taken a hold on him. I don't see that as being anything but good for Rangers!

2 March 1989

We announced from Ibrox that Alan Montgomery who has been a top executive with Scottish Television is joining Rangers as chief executive. At last a signing which hasn't been made by me and which hasn't cost a big transfer fee – though that is also to come this week! Alan's appointment has been discussed between David and myself and it is in an area where we feel the club could be strengthened. Essentially a football club in these modern times has to have management on two levels. There has to be the management or the coaching at the ground roots' level, running the team, buying the players, signing young players, getting a youth system in place, and generally controlling the playing side at Ibrox. On the other level we have to have a management team to operate in the other administrative areas. If we are to compete with the AC Milans and Barcelonas and Bayern Munichs then we must have revenue coming in from sources other than gate revenue.

I believe this will be a vital addition to the Ibrox team. In fact, Alan could prove every bit as important as any of the big money players we have bought. He is the man who has to bring in extra cash to sustain our challenge and to help us towards our objectives. We have made massive investments in players and that money is being pushed back into the club through the turnstiles. The fans have helped us finance the buying of players – but all of it cannot come from the supporters. We have to have other major sources of income and Alan Montgomery will be finding these for us. All the top clubs in Europe have incredible funding from outside the game – we have to follow suit. It is the way ahead for all of us. I think that Alan will provide sponsorship packages which will enable us to continue to field the very best players at Ibrox.

The fans want quality after all and we have tried to provide that. We have to keep on doing so because of the demand to see the top names. But quality costs money and between Alan's endeavours on one side and the support we have had from the fans on the other we will be able to maintain our very high standards.

3 March 1989

We get Mel Sterland at last. All the little delays have held up the deal but the signing we thought might take place two or three weeks ago has now gone though. It has cost the club £750,000 but we have another English international player and we have someone who can slot into various areas for us. There are a lot of tough games ahead in the Premier League and in the Scottish Cup and he is available for all of them. That is the crucial thing. And with no Premier League games tomorrow because of the World Cup game in midweek Mel has a chance to settle, to find his feet before making his debut.

He will find it difficult to adjust to the pace of the game. Every player who has come north to play for Rangers has found that. He won't be any exception and the week will give him a little bit of time to get himself ready for what will be something of a culture shock as far as football is concerned. The speed and ferocity of the game in the Premier League – especially the games we are involved in – takes a bit of getting used to.

30 March 1989

Another anouncement from Ibrox. This time David is spelling out his plans for the stadium. He knows that we have been operating on a gates-shut basis for a large part of the season. He believes that increasing the capacity would help us. It will cost £10 million but he is ready to charge ahead with his plans because he believes in this club's future. I told you – he is as consumed by the club as we all are!

The capacity will increase to more than 52,000 and a new tier will be built on the stand. As well as that, executive boxes will be built in the close season and will be available to the public very soon. In fact, half of them have been bought already. That is in

Mel Sterland had a short stay only at Ibrox – but he did help the team take the title!

the first phase of the development. The second phase will bring more executive boxes at a cost of £50,000 each. There the owners can entertain their guests to a meal inside and then step out on to a terrace to watch the game. The terraces will, of course, be heated. David heard about this concept from a friend who had been at the racecourse in Hong Kong. He latched on to it and had it built into the Ibrox plans. The man misses nothing. I thought we had the best stadium in the country and here he is ready to improve it and enlarge it. He knows what he is doing. This is his business and he will make it all work. The enclosure will be kept because we still have a loyal support who do want to stand and so we keep the area. But the seating capacity will increase to 45,000. It is an important announcement and a special Ibrox bond will allow the fans to have their names on their own seats in the new tier. Again this will be a winner and the cash raised from this will help finance the improvements.

As we announce this new expenditure Alan Montgomery also pledges that the overdraft will soon be taken care of. Certainly it will be easier to do so now that the buying is slowing down. We knew that would happen – it would have to happen – but there was no way to avoid it when we first took over. Walter and I looked at the squad of players we had and right away knew that only major surgery would push us towards the success the club wanted. And the victories the fans demanded. It could not have been done without the major investments in players we made at that time.

But now we see ourselves as being closer to the kind of squad we want. When we arrived we could have bought something like 200 players – all of whom would have improved on what we had. If we were to buy now, there are only perhaps 20 players who would improve us. I believe that. In fact I know that it is true. This is the third season we are in and each season I have noticed an improvement. This time it has been helped because we have been able to play a settled team – so unlike the season before when suspensions and injuries wrecked so many of our dreams. We went out of Europe when we might have gone further than that quarter-final place against Steaua of Bucharest. We dropped out of the Scottish Cup again to a sucker punch from

Dunfermline. And, above all, we lost the title we had won in our first season. Maybe that victory had come a little early – but it was the one we had wanted to build on and we were not able to do that.

Now we are on another phase of our plans and we will have a team to match the super stadium which is soon to be ready. The investment in that will match the investment in star players and the fans will have comfort off the field and, hopefully, entertainment on it. There is a little bit of showbiz about Ibrox now and I like that. But whether I like it or not hardly matters. What really counts is that the fans like it. Just look at the gates again this season and try to tell me anything different! We must be doing something right despite the niggling criticisms we seem always to have to contend with.

14 April 1989

The semi-final of the Scottish Cup is tomorrow and when David Murray and I meet that is the main topic of conversation over the table. The last two Premier League games have been important for us and leave us still clear at the top, while the Scottish Cup provides a break from the long hard League campaign.

Things have settled down after the takeover and the announcement of the new developments at the stadium. That was something David had obviously had in mind before he was signing the deal with Lawrence Marlborough. That is, after all, the type of person he is. He does not rest at all. His mind is always active, he is always planning ahead. Basically, even I wonder what he is going to get up to next. He won't sit back and rest. That is not his way. But it convinces me still further that he is the right man to have in charge of the club. I know that he sees the upgrading of the stadium and the bonds scheme as something tangible for the supporters, something that will last for their lifetime and for his lifetime and something that brings them even closer to being a part of the club. But, more important, he never loses sight of the one thing that the supporters want more than anything else – and that is Glasgow Rangers being successful on the field. It is out there on the park that the fans want to see the fruits of any takeover deal. We are all aware of that.

The stadium is the best in Britain – and that is even before the work has been carried out to add the boxes and the new tier with the personalised seats. But that apart, David Murray will make Rangers one of the best and biggest clubs in Europe. Whether I will be there all along the road helping him to do that, I don't know. As I pointed out earlier, a run of bad results can get me the sack just as it can get any manager the sack. Or we could have a fall-out – and these things do happen in life.

I would like to think that I will be there because I don't want to leave this club. It would be my hope that in 30 years' time my shares will be passed on to my two sons. It would be good to think that would happen – because by then this club will be the finest ever seen in Britain. David will make it that. You only have to sit with him and listen to him as I do each Friday to realise that. His mind is never at rest. Always he is thinking ahead, planning ahead, and you simply cannot keep pace with him. For the Rangers' supporters he is the best thing to have happened to Rangers Football Club for a long, long time – probably in their lifetimes.

David Murray is a wealthy, wealthy man, which goes without saying, I suppose. But it is not the money which is important to him. He wants to be successful in everything he does and to have that success he surrounds himself with bright, intelligent people. He is tremendously bright himself and the people who are working for him or with him are the same. Successful people want to be in his company because they get sparks back from him – just as he does from them. Anything he learns he stores away and then he will use it in one or other of his projects. The idea of the terraces outside the boxes is an example I mentioned earlier. Some friend of his had been at the new racetrack in Hong Kong, seen them there – and David knew immediately this was what he wanted for Ibrox. It makes the stadium different from any of the others in Britain, or maybe Europe, and he jumped in straight away to have the terraces planned. It frightens you at times, the way he operates, because you can never predict what he will do next. All that is predictable is that it will be of benefit to the club. Either on the field or off the field.

I came to the conclusion some time ago that the fact that he has so many good operators around him isn't luck. He doesn't

A new look Graeme Souness showed up at Ibrox after his summer break – the Boss was sporting a beard.

rely on luck. It is all down to his own good judgment. He is listening all the time. And learning all the time. He has everything at his fingertips. It is frightening. But good for Rangers.

9 June 1989

Another Ibrox press conference and this time Alan Montgomery can let the media know of a new strip deal we have finalised with Admiral. It will not take place for another year, until our present contract ends, but it is an important step for the club because it is the biggest-ever deal for any club in Britain. We will have £4 million for the five-year term and it is an early sign of the sponsorship stakes being increased.

Alan spells things out to the press. He tells them bluntly that sponsorship is needed to match so many of the continental clubs who are talking of the Super League. He cites the backing of AC Milan by Berlusconi, the Italian media mogul; how Opel, the giant car firm, backs Bayern Munich; how Philips are the company behind PSV Eindhoven – and there are others, too. All the time, though, he stresses how Rangers have to be ready to face the fresh challenges which will be thrown up by Europe. That is a situation I have long been aware of – and the Admiral deal will not be the last. It cannot be, because Rangers cannot sit still waiting for deals to fall into our laps. We have to pursue them and we have to look for opportunities and then grasp them. It is the only way. The upgrading of Ibrox has to be paid for and so do new players.

Yesterday I agreed on a signing deal with Trevor Steven and that will cost us more than one million pounds. But it was a move we had contemplated for a long time, and if it needs underlined just how the power in the game is being switched around, we were able to beat off several of the top clubs in the English First Division to get the player. Deals like the one today help finance the playing staff as well as the improvements to the ground. It all has to be seen together, to be looked at together, and the bottom line has always to be keeping the supporters happy. That means top-quality players and top-quality surroundings in which to watch the stars. To me that would seem an unbeatable combination. But we have to continue to work hard on all levels to finance the package. Europe remains that elusive dream and we have to get ourselves involved with the big guns because that is where this club belongs!

It is also what our fans deserve. They want to see the best and part of our duty to them is to give them that opportunity. Knowing David, he won't fail them. He hasn't missed out on too much with regard to success in any other areas. I don't see football being a first for him.

The ferocity of the Premier League is shown here as Derek Ferguson and, in the background, Davie Kirkwood try to stop Dundee United veteran Paul Hegarty in this aerial duel.

3

Signings. Football Should Be Showbiz

Most of the headline grabbing done by Rangers under Graeme Souness has been because of his wheeling and dealing in the transfer market. No one in Scotland has ever spent as much. No one in Scotland has ever been able to attract such star names into the game north of the border. There is no doubt that the personal charisma of Souness has brought players such as Terry Butcher, Gary Stevens, Trevor Steven and others to Ibrox. Equally, Souness knew that he had to buy the best and he had to go beyond his own country's borders to get the men he wanted. He has a theory about the buying and selling of players which he outlines here to give another insight into the manager who has changed the game in Scotland out of all recognition from the parish pump League it was before. Souness believes the game is part of showbiz. Watching the success he has had it's difficult to argue with that.

6 May 1989

After the game against Dundee at Dens Park I'm asked about spending big money and I tell the newspapermen there that I would love to be able to field a team of all-Scottish players one day. I would – but I don't know if that will ever be possible for Rangers now. The way we are heading, the direction we have been taking, is putting us into the very top bracket of clubs. To be there you have to have the very best players and so to have a team of nothing but Scots you are looking at having the entire Scotland international team playing for one club. I don't see that ever happening. It is a nice thought but if you want to be the best then you have to have the best players you can get. That means that we will be developing as many young Scottish players as we can – but always we have to leave the gate open for players from other countries.

The public only want to go to see the best films now. The public only want to buy the best clothes or drive the best cars. That is how they are conditioned now. That is how they look at life. They are looking for quality and in football we have to give them quality just as other areas of showbusiness give them that quality. If there is a Super League then so be it – it is what the people want. I believe that people want the best things in life when they are available. The game is going forward and we are going forward with it.

There is a lot of talk about limiting teams to a certain number of foreign players. It will affect our forward planning if it goes through – and we won't be alone. All the top clubs in Europe and a lot of the lesser clubs in France and Italy, for example, and Belgium, too, will be hit by a ruling which stops too many foreign players turning out in European Cup games. In our case we would be hit because the English lads are tagged 'foreigners'. I don't think this is a good thing for the game. Of course, people will say that I would take that stance because I am with Rangers and because I launched the programme of buying big name English players. OK, they are entitled to that view – but that is not the reason for my saying this. If I was not involved with Rangers then I would say the same.

At Liverpool one season we won the European Cup with just three English players in the team. The great Real Madrid team would have been weakened by this rule. So many of the top teams would have been lessened if this ruling had been in force. It goes back to what I said – people want the best. They are not going to concern themselves too much over the nationality of the players. Did Real Madrid fans worry that Puskas was Hungarian or that Di Stefano was Argentinian? Were Juventus fans worried that Platini was French and Boniek was Polish? I don't think so because they were seeing the best players and they were playing for their team. They could turn up in Turin and the Stadio Communale and watch Platini entertain them. Just as the Napoli fans turn out to see Maradona and never tire of watching him. No amount of legislation – which seems to be aimed at a levelling down in the game – would wipe out the memories that these fans have of their heroes. I like to think that Rangers' fans will look back on some of the players I have brought here and think the same in years to come. It would be nice to think that you have provided a few dreams and a few magic moments for the people who support the team.

Yes, it would be nice to have an all-Scottish side. But maybe the possibility has disappeared. We will step up our youth policy. It will soon be paying dividends and we will have a flow of young homegrown players – but there are times when every big club has to buy. And buy big. The public demand that.

I think we have done a lot to push Rangers' name back into the forefront of this game. People of my generation all across the world recognised Rangers as leaders in the game. Then I think there were years when that fell away and so youngsters were thinking about Manchester United or Liverpool or Nottingham Forest or Celtic or whatever. I hope that we have reversed that trend in the past three seasons and we want to continue to do that.

There is no way we are going to simply look at these rules and then walk away from the policy we have. People today want the best, just as I've said. And they want it in a sports context as much as anything else. It is entertainment. They only want the best tennis, the best golf and in these games you have almost a travelling circus going around the world. But it is the top people in these sports that people want to watch. It will happen in football too because of the explosion of satellite television and the way that air travel is making the world smaller and smaller. We have to be prepared for it and that will take the best players.

The first thrust of the English invasion – Chris Woods, Graham Roberts and Terry Butcher line up with boss Souness and former chairman David Holmes.

I have had to take a lot of stick about spending millions of pounds on players. Every time I make a big buy then it's "Souness has now hit new records in the transfer market" or words to that effect. Eight million pounds, ten million pounds – take your pick, these are the figures being bandied around and no one thinks of the other side of the coin. No one points out that we have also sold a whole lot of players. At the last count the sales going out of Ibrox had reached around three million pounds. However, that isn't what people want to read. They want to know about the flash Harry, the big spender, the high roller, the guy who is ready to splash out millions on player after player, on star after star.

But what I want to do is give the supporters the best team in Britain. I think they deserve that. It annoys me when people talk about us buying the title or buying success. If I had stood by the players who were there when I took over at Ibrox then they might still have been there – but I would not. I would have been sacked because with the players who were there I would not have won anything! I didn't have any alternative when I stepped into the job. I had to buy and I had to buy quality and there was no other way. Believe me. I am not interested in critics of Rangers. I am interested in the people who support this club. If I can do right by them then I'll be happy – and I'm sure they will let me know when I let them down.

But I don't intend to let them down, because since I came to Ibrox they have never let me or the players down. They have turned up in their thousands and we all know how many sacrifices they make to be able to back us. None of us at the club forgets that.

We carry a burden by being Rangers – people look for our result at times, hoping to see us beaten. One half of the country looks to see if we have won, the other half looks for the result hoping we have lost. I have spent money but we have also stimulated interest in the game all through the country. People turn out to see Terry Butcher. Or maybe they will want to catch Mark Walters because he is an entertainer. Or Ray Wilkins because he is a cultured, skilful midfield player. I like to think we have attracted people back to this game. I'm not looking for pats on the back from other clubs – because I only want to see Rangers winning. But no one can deny the interest we have created. Full houses wherever we play – can that be bad for the game in Scotland? I doubt it.

As for spending millions of pounds on players, I have only one worry over that – I want the deals to be good ones because the money I spend comes from the fans and it should be spent on giving them the kind of team they want. And the success they want.

The man who owns this club now and the people round about him will give them the best team in Britain. I would like to be here when that happens. I hope that I am here but if I'm not then another manager will take over and with David Murray here that dream of being the best will become reality. It's my dream too because I don't want to leave. Ever. Only failure will move me out of the manager's office at Ibrox.

5 June 1989

Hopefully we will soon know whether Trevor Steven joins us and I'm anxious that he will because he is the kind of player we have been looking for almost since the day we started rebuilding the side here. That wide position on the right which Trevor handles better than anyone else in the game has been a problem spot for us. If he comes it is solved. I'll hear about the big spending again but, as I have said before, this club needs big names and big names cost big money. I still get a little thrill out of the fact that so many people come to watch us – even if they are turning up on a Saturday afternoon hoping to see us lose it doesn't matter. What counts is that we have helped get them out of their homes and along to the ground to watch a football match. I get a kick out of that.

There has to be a showbusiness touch about the game and it was only when I went to Italy that I could fully appreciate that. I spent seven years at Liverpool, probably the most professional club in Britain, and then I went to play in Italy in what has to be the best league in Europe – possibly the world. And at Anfield everything was football and nothing else mattered. The media,

Bargain buy, Ray Wilkins, whose return from the continent was a Souness coup.

newspapers or televison, anything outside the game itself, didn't get a mention. It was just the game. Just football and a 100 per cent concentration on that. It was all I knew and so when I went to Italy I had my eyes opened. It's the opposite there – and their game doesn't suffer because of the publicity which surrounds it. It blossoms, in fact. It thrives on all the glitz and glamour which surrounds every game that is played over there. It is pure theatre and the fans love it. I learned that this is the way it is always done and has always been done and I like to think I learned a little more from my spell with Sampdoria.

They come to see the manager tearing his hair out on the touchline... .

They come to see the fans unfurling the biggest flag in Europe, which Sampdoria boasted their fans possessed... .

They come to see the biggest names in the game – be it Van Basten or Gullitt or Maradona or Careca or Matthaus or their own exceptionally good players... .

They come to see the fireworks... .

They even come to see the famous referee... .

That is the way it is over there. It is so marvellously theatrical without ever losing sight of the main aim which has to be the same with every club and that is finding success on the field. That has left its mark on me. I don't think there is any doubt about that. Deep down I am still the Liverpool-trained person who does not want anything to interfere with the thorough professionalism that was drilled into me in those seven years at Anfield. But I am also very much aware that we have to be involved in the publicity machine. So we have to pay attention to that and we have to be equipped to match the top Europeans when it comes to projecting ourselves, be it with buying star players or whatever.

But we still cannot lose sight of the fact that we have to win that Premier League. I have said that before and I make no apologies for repeating it. Losing the League could cost me my job. It has to be the prize you aim for every season. It is no use spending loadsamoney on players who will help you win in Europe if these same players cannot handle the special challenges thrown up by the game here at home. There is a vast difference between competing in Europe against the continentals and battling away at home against the other teams who are chasing the prizes just as much as you are.

It can be done – Liverpool did it for years and years because they had a compromise situation which suited them and the players who were there in my time. They had a good, solid professional backbone but also they had some of the best individuals in the British game. They probably had four or five who were absolutely, without any question, the best in their positions in the whole country. But that did not come into it. What was most important was that they were willing to put their personal skills towards the team effort. They subdued them, at times, so that the general team play would benefit. And that way Liverpool had the best of both worlds. Dalglish, McDermott, Phil Neal, Hansen – they were the best in their positions as far as I'm concerned. But that just went out of the window because they would sacrifice all their skills for the team. Any individual thoughts were abandoned. In this way we were able to vary from the very competitive style we had to use at home – because that is what the British public demand – to a more continental approach. Against the continentals, we would settle down and start to play passes and often play the Europeans off the park! We could do that. Just as if we had turned on a switch. And that is what we will have to try to do at Ibrox as well.

You have to be able to change the style of play. The first 20 minutes or so in our football is a battle, then you can get into a real game of football. That is why I have been spending so much time striving to get our playing surface right. I believe that the better the surfaces we play on then the greater chance we have of doing well. The playing surface at Ibrox has been a problem for me since day one here and now we hope that we have been able to solve this. I was criticised last season because I opened my mouth and let off steam about some of the pitches we are asked to play on but it's true. Our own pitch was not right. We are attempting now to make that better for the future. If other teams don't want to do that then that is their prerogative. But I'm trying to get our pitch in perfect condition because that is the surface which will allow the best football. I want it as near perfect for passing as possible. I want it like the Liverpool pitch.

Or the Everton pitch. Or the Nottingham Forest pitch. The game is constantly changing – but that is one aspect which doesn't change. Good passing movements, good passing skills will win games. And they will also entertain the public. I hope this time our changes will work out well enough so that we can boast about the standard of the surface at Ibrox. It is the way forward for us.

Of course there are other aspects of the modern game, aspects which have come in since I was playing at top level. I think there is a greater need for athleticism in the new breed of player– more than there was when I was, say, at Liverpool. You need players who can get themselves up and down that field right through the 90 minutes of every game. These are the players who win you games. More and more you have to look to them and their running power to bring you success. Thankfully we have our share of that type of player.

Anyhow, if the Steven deal goes through it will be another big one, but David Murray knows I want the player and we have talked the matter through. He leaves that up to me, though if too many mistakes were made in buying players he would be the first to say, ''You have got this wrong'' – and I accept that. It has to be that way. This time, though, I know the money we have available for team strengthening and David knows we need the squad improved. All we need is for the boy to say yes.

Big clubs will always have to buy but if I can get Trevor Steven and maybe another deal or two that we have been considering then I could be looking at a team for the next four years. FOUR YEARS. So the spending which was essential to get to that stage will be over. Or certainly curtailed.

It has never worried me that I have spent big money. However many millions of pounds it may now have reached, it is not something I lose sleep over because it has been necessary for the development of this club. If it stacks up financially then you go for it. There isn't any other way. No big club today will win all the prizes by relying on a conveyor belt of homegrown talent. All you can hope for is a mix of the two – partly homegrown, partly bought – and then put it all together and see how the mix works. When we start off next season the quality of player available at Rangers will be far, far ahead of anything I dreamed possible when I stepped into the job. But that still doesn't guarantee us any prizes.

The thing which gives me satisfaction is that we have been able to rebuild the team, change the entire set-up – and still win trophies. In the three years there has been an enormous turnover in personnel and yet we have been able twice to win the title – and I still see that as the blue riband – and the Skol Cup three times. We can take a lot of pleasure from that. Normally clubs who are rebuilding have a fallow period, a time when they re-assess and try to get back to finding success with fresh players. We have been able to have success as we brought in fresh faces. It has been very gratifying for myself and Walter Smith and Phil Boersma and all the other members of the backroom staff.

4

The Transfer Whirl

As well as buying players for Rangers, Souness has also been involved in selling them. His constant moves in the transfer market are always aimed at making Rangers a better team. He also realises that sometimes transfer deals have to be financed by selling off players to make room for others coming in. He has spent millions of pounds – he has also taken in millions of pounds. Here he gives an insight into some of the deals last season, takes time off to explain the row with Graham Roberts which ended with the player being banished to the reserves and then sold to Chelsea, and reveals how he eventually clinched the signing of Trevor Steven for a record transfer fee of £1,525,000. It was the biggest fee ever paid by a Scottish club and the largest ever set by a transfer tribunal.

11 July 1988

The opening spell of training at Ibrox is over and here we are ready to start the really hard work at Il Ciocco. This is where I trained pre-season when I was with Sampdoria. The complex has everything we need, plus sunshine we would not have at home. The lads will enjoy it – those who are with us. They can work and they can relax and they won't have any of the distractions they would have at home. It is ideal and yet there are problems which have to be resolved. I am still trying to finalise the deal which will bring Gary Stevens to join us. And as a hangover from last season we still have the Graham Roberts business to sort out. In one sense it is finalised – he is leaving. But we do not want the hassle we had at the end of last season when he turned up at Falkirk after being dropped and caused the club embarrassment. This is the last thing we need and it is something we want to avoid.

Robbo knows the score. He has not trained with the first-team squad and we have left him at home while we are here in Italy. Nothing will happen until we go back. But the fact that he asked for a transfer and the fact that we decided to give him what he wanted makes it essential that he trains away from the first-team pool of players. He will not be a part of our plans in the future and therefore I do not see the point of his being involved in any of the pre-season preparations. I don't care about any flak I may get. That is a decision based on what is best for the players who will be staying with this club – players who are leaving don't concern me.

Still, the whole thing has to be resolved and as quickly as possible. But there is no way that any club will walk in and get Robbo on the cheap because we have had a row. They will have to meet my asking price. When one of them does that, then he can go – and obviously he will be playing in England next season. In some ways it is a pity because he did do a job for us in the first season he joined the club. But there is no use looking back on that. You have to look forward in this game and he is leaving. That is the bottom line for myself and Walter as we get this squad ready for the new season. The club is always bigger than any single player. It has to be.

29 July 1988

Back home and the first of the pre-season games comes up tomorrow at Kirkcaldy. It is against Raith Rovers who gave us a fright in the Scottish Cup last season. It is a fair old test and it will give the players a nice run in towards what they have to

Graham Roberts and Graeme Souness in happier times – before the dressing-room bust up saw the hard man defender sold to Chelsea.

face this year. Frank Connor won't allow us to relax. Nothing will be easy and that is the way it has to be.

Robbo won't be with us. He will go with a second team to another fixture. We have had an offer from Chelsea but it is not what we want and we have told them that. He would be a good player for them. They want back to the First Division and Robbo would help them get there – but he is not going cheaply. They are looking to pinch him because they know there has been bother. There is no way that will happen. I have a figure in mind. When they reach that then they can get the player. I am not going to make this transfer some kind of giveaway. No one should think we are soft marks at Ibrox. We are not. When we go for players we have to pay the going rate – or, more often, above the going rate. Why should others be treated differently when they want our players? I don't get it. And they won't get Robbo! He is not leaving because of a lack of ability. He is leaving because of other reasons and if they need the player – and I can understand why they want him – then they will have to come up to my price.

31 July 1988

Predictably the newspapers have had a field day on the Robbo business because he is with the reserve side. Well, it won't alter things. He will stay with them. I know that he is popular with the fans. I know he became a hero to them in the 18 months he was in the first team and helping us win the title and then the Skol Cup. But I am the manager and it is my privilege and my prerogative to handle awkward situations in MY way. I cannot allow myself to be influenced by what the supporters think in every case. Things don't work that way. They never have. If there is flak then I have to take it. That is why I am the manager. I may not always be right. In fact, I know that I cannot possibly be right all the time. But this time I am right. I know that I am.

In the last game of the season against Aberdeen we lost a diabolical goal and after the game I told the players that. I also told Robbo that it was his fault. We had a row in the dressing-room. Not as bad a row as rumours made it out to be. Call it a

One of the Scottish stars in Rangers' multi-million pounds all-Britain team – Richard Gough, who remains one of the manager's best signings.

frank and fearless exchange of views if you like. But he put me into a position where I could not back down. If I had then I would not have had a future with this club.

I have never been one to walk away from any confrontation in any case. And Robbo is not the kind of person who turns his back when there is trouble. But I could not allow him to win. If I had then I could not have continued as manager – because I would not have done my job. It was a straightforward choice for me – either he went or my head was on the chopping block. That was not going to happen. I had to win and I did and I will continue to handle this job the way I want to handle it. There is not any other way. Not for me. And not for any manager who is worth his salt. Robbo will continue to train with the reserves and play for the reserves if that is what I decide. No one is going to change my mind. I could not afford that. If I get stick from the fans then so be it. But they have to realise that I am paid to be the manager and while their views concern me they cannot influence me all the time – especially when, in this case, they don't know the facts.

7 August 1988

At last the Robbo saga is reaching an end. Chelsea have been on again and this time they have reached the £450,000 figure I had in mind. He is on his way back to London and, in many ways, I'm sure that is where he wanted to go. Home again!

Now that it is over I can sit back and look at the contribution he made. I have a lot of respect for Robbo. I still do even though it has ended with a little bit of acrimony. He came up here and he did a great job for me and for the club. I can hold no grudges against him. I have a lot of admiration for him as regards what he did in that first season. He helped propel us towards the title because he arrived at that stage of the season when it is getting harder and harder for the players to keep going, just at the turn of the year. He was brought in and he helped us take that championship. I will always thank him for that. But that was 18 months before our row and he has to realise that in that one I was right.

*Former days for a new Ibrox hero – Mo Johnston in action
AGAINST Rangers for Celtic. Chris Woods smothers the ball
as former Ranger Graham Roberts races in and Terry Butcher
watches anxiously.*

I hope there is no bad blood between us. I would not like to think there is. If Robbo looks at what happened now he has had a little time to reflect, then he must say to himself that he put me in an impossible position. Maybe he won't see that now. Maybe it will take him a little longer. Maybe when he is a little older, maybe when he is a manager himself he will see that he gave me no alternative. Perhaps that won't be the view he holds now – but when he is a little older, a little wiser, then I'm sure he will see that. It was him or me – and I wasn't ready to go!

27 June 1988

We are ready to clinch the signing of Kevin Drinkell. We are going to get him for £500,000 and that looks a good deal to me. It is only a year ago that they were looking for a million pounds for him. He is a good professional and he will give us that little bit of added dig up front. We had problems there last season when Ally McCoist was asked to do a lot on his own. This is something we have thought about – and other deals are on the way. We have spoken to Everton about Gary Stevens as well and we are waiting to hear from Colin Harvey about that one. Again, it is something we have had planned. I think that people get the impression that we simply rush in waving a cheque book when a good player becomes available. It is not as simplistic as that. You have to look at players over a period of time. You have to see them in action time after time. You have to look at how they react to certain situations, how they respond when that little bit extra is demanded of them.

Walter and Phil Boersma and myself discuss ways of strengthening the team all the time. You can't sit still thinking you have done it and you don't need anything else and that you can't improve on what you have got available. That day never arrives. Once you get to thinking that way then you run the danger of complacency setting in and that is a dangerous commodity to have around a football club. You have to strive always to improve and if that means running tabs on all the good players around then you do it. You don't leap into deals willy-

Joint top scorers in Scotland in season 1988–89 – Ally McCoist and Kevin Drinkell.

nilly because someone is up for grabs. You have to know the player you are buying inside out. You have to know what kind of fellow he is off the field. You have to know what kind of background he comes from. What kind of family life he leads. Every tiny detail comes into play because as well as buying a good player you have to hope that you are buying someone who will fit into the club. You cannot simply buy what you see – you have to look behind that on-field image too.

You have to remember that I am in there spending a million pounds – maybe even more than a million pounds – of our supporters' money. That is where the cash to buy players comes from. It comes from the fans who dig deep into their pockets week after week during every season to support us. So when I am spending big money on transfers I know that I have to try to get it right.

OK, you cannot always get it right. But most of the time I try to. And in the past any mistakes which I have made in the transfer market have been corrected. If a player has not fitted in then I have been able to sell him on. It has happened with Colin West and Neil Woods and Mark Falco and if it has to happen with others then that is the way of things. But to be a good manager I have to get deals right most of the time. So far I think I'm ahead of the game.

I reckon few people would argue with the big money signings I have made. Most clubs would want Chris Woods or Terry Butcher or Richard Gough or Ray Wilkins or Mark Walters around. I think the two lads I'm chasing now will turn out to be as good as any of them. Their value will be equal in team terms even though they may not appear to be. In this instance the defender, Gary Stevens, is going to be a bigger signing in cash terms than the striker, Kevin Drinkell. That is not the usual way of things. But to me they will each add something distinctive to the squad of players we are gathering around us. They were both on our wanted list and that list is only drawn up after severe scrutiny of each player on it.

Striker Kevin Drinkell and boss Souness after winning the Player and Manager of the Month awards in Scotland.

29 June 1988

D-day for signing number one. Kevin Drinkell is now a Rangers player and, as I noted yesterday, he will give Coisty the kind of support he didn't always have last year. I think the fans will take to the new boy. He is a complete professional. A thorough 100 per cent trier who gets his share of goals but can be unselfish enough to lay things off for his front line mates. He is strong, good in the air and difficult for any defender to knock off the ball. Maybe he is not international class, maybe he is not looked on as a possible England player – but he will do me. You cannot have a team filled with stars, you need the work-horses too. You need the good, solid, experienced professionals. They will always be the important cogs in any team. And usually they are the kind of players the fans eventually take to. Often they can be unsung heroes – but Rangers' supporters love a trier. Kevin is that and more. It has taken us a little while to get him – he was targetted some time ago. But he is in now and at the right time and the right price.

It is a problem solved up front and that will allow us to play Ian Ferguson in the midfield role he prefers. It is also where he is best. We could not always do that last season and the boy didn't complain, but he suffered a little. Now he won't have to. All we are waiting for is the Gary Stevens deal. It would be nice to have that tied up before we left for Tuscany and the pre-season training there. But that is probably expecting too much. Getting the player for the start of the season is the really vital thing. This is a crucial signing for us if we can pull it off... .

13 July 1988

I spoke to Colin Harvey from Il Ciocco today and everything is OK. He has accepted our offer. It is one million pounds, but for that we are buying someone of real international quality. And again it is a player we have chased for some time now. Somehow you just don't believe that you are going to get this type of player readily. It was the fact that he was unhappy at Goodison which gave us the opportunity to move in. He had been there since he was a boy and he was restless. He thought he needed a change.

I worked out arrangements with Colin Harvey to speak to the
boy. It might have been done earlier in the summer but for the
European Championships. Gary had been playing for England
in West Germany and so it was all held up until the pre-season
period.

Gary will fly into Pisa Airport as soon as a flight can be
arranged. He will be our player and he will be able to work
out with the lads here in Il Ciocco. He can get an understanding
going with the other defenders and we will be another step
closer to that settled back four Walter and I have dreamed of
since taking over. Injuries and other circumstances have forced
us to chop and change and that is not the way to win trophies,
not the way to get the kind of success that we are looking for.
You have to be right at the back. You have to be secure there
and then build from that. A proper foundation is essential and
in any of the great teams that foundation is the defence. Pro-
viding our talks go without any hitches at the airport tomorrow,
then we will have him in at right-back, big Terry back at the
centre of the defence alongside Richard Gough and we are on the
right road. This will make me happy with the close season deal-
ings. God, don't let there be any unforeseen problems. I don't
need any.

14 July 1988

No snags! Gary agreed terms at the airport and immediately he
came up to Il Ciocco and settled in nicely at training. I feel now
that if Gary shows his true form with us then that side of our
defence is taken care of for a long, long time to come. I look on
him as being the best defender in Britain. He has his critics. They
don't think he uses the ball well enough when he gets forward.
But I bought him to sit in there in the right-back position. And
I'll ask anyone to show me players who get past him. On the odd
occasion that they do then he has the pace to get back at them.
He is the ideal modern defender. Quick. Athletic. Strong. He
gets tight on his opponent, he can get across to cover and he is
the best at reading the situation. I think he edges ahead of

Richard Gough as the best defender in the whole country – and everyone knows what I think of Goughie.

This is going to prove one of my best signings. I can hardly wait to see how it all settles in. Every manager's dream is to have a settled team. You want to have long-term aims in that direction – particularly at the back. You look at Aberdeen and you see Alex McLeish and Willie Miller and then at Dundee United you have had Paul Hegarty and Dave Narey and these partnerships have been together for season after season, forming the basis of their club's successes over these seasons. That is what you always want to have. Maybe this is going to lead to that kind of settled look at our place. If you can get a back four you can rely on, one where the understanding is right and the ability cannot be questioned, then you are halfway to achieving real success in the game. No one can ever have a whole team. That is beyond any manager's dreams. But if you get one of the units, or even two of the units, spot on you are there!

At Liverpool the last thing the bench would ever do was substitute a defender. They never wanted to disturb things at the back. Even if one of the players at the back was having a total nightmare they would leave it alone because they reckoned they were used to playing together and that counted for more than individual lapses on the day.

That is what we are striving for. We want to be able to look at that back four and see it working as a unit. If they are going to push up and play people offside then they have to do that together. One player misses the signal and you are caught. So the understanding has to be there and that comes through experience of playing together. And when you have the added bonus of quality players in these positions then you have won a watch. It is so different from what you are looking for further up the park. You can have Mark Walters up there and he will give you entertainment and individual genius and the little bit extra that forwards can provide for the fans. But a back four have to think as a unit and operate like one. It is the only way and we will be close to that now that we have Gary. People will criticise the money we have spent. Let them. I want someone in there who will say to me, "Thanks, Boss, for buying me, now relax because

Gary Stevens, the "best defender in Britain", says Souness, in action against St Mirren.

you won't get any problems down this side of the field.'' My money is on Gary Stevens to give me that security. I would not have bought him otherwise.

13 August 1988

Debut day for Gary Stevens and Kevin Drinkell and it is away from home at Hamilton. Hardly the place I would have picked for them to play their first game. But at the end of it Gary has scored and Kevin has played well and things look fine. Drinks and Coisty look as if they will work well together and the defence had a solid look that we never had last season. Then, because of the constant changes, we were always looking to lose goals. I don't think that will be a worry for us too often this season. Money well spent, I'd say!

11 October 1988

We have gone a dozen games, including several in the Skol Cup and one in the UEFA Cup as well as those in the Premier League. Maybe it's time for a progress report on the new boys – and I'm delighted with the way both of them have responded. Kevin has scored five goals, including one in his first Old Firm game against Celtic at Ibrox. Gary has scarcely put a foot wrong. But, then, it's what I was looking for at the start of the season, a settled defence.

We have made the odd change at left-back where Stuart Munro and John Brown have shared the position but the other three places have gone to Gary, Richard Gough and Terry Butcher. In the dozen games we have lost only four goals. That is the type of security which sends any team towards a title. It is early, of course, but there is still some satisfaction to be taken from the way the lads have performed and especially the new players. The doubters have had to stay quiet.

13 May 1989

The last League game of the season and it's against Aberdeen at Ibrox. It doesn't matter except in terms of pride because the title has been won. But for Gary Stevens the year is almost over and he misses his first match of the season because he took a little bit of a knock at Dens Park a week ago. He has been a revelation – even better than I expected – and I have acknowledged that by giving him a new five-year contract. We started talking about a fresh deal after he had been with the club for just six months. It's the long-term future I see as important and by keeping him here for five years it means he will be a Rangers player for the rest of his career. That is how highly I rate his contribution this year. As for the other major buy who came at the same time, Kevin Drinkell, just look at his goalscoring record and you'll find him at the top alongside Ally McCoist and Mark McGhee of Celtic. You could not ask for much more from either of them. Nineteen goals is more than I ever expected from Kevin. What I did expect, of course, was that the fans would take to him. I was totally right about that.

3 March 1989

I have been tracking Mel Sterland for several weeks now and a change of manager at Sheffield Wednesday didn't help us. But now the deal is on and going through and we have the player, which is the most important thing of all. I played against Mel a few times when I was down there and I know what he can do. He can be a valuable addition to the pool.

It is no secret that we need quality cover. And we need it even more just now because Terry is within one booking of what would be a four-game suspension. It doesn't bear thinking about that we could have come this far along the road towards the title and then lose because of suspension or injury. Mel can slot into any of the defensive areas for us or play in midfield. Originally I was negotiating with Peter Eustace and we reached agreement with him. Then he was sacked and we had to start all over again with Ron Atkinson before we came to another agreement. It's done though and Mel, who can be right-back or right midfield, mainly, can play his part in helping us get the title.

11 March 1989

Mel Sterland makes his debut at right midfield with young Tommy Cowan making his first appearance at full-back in this game against Hamilton at Ibrox. Mel scores and I hope this helps him settle. He found it difficult to adjust to the pace of the game and he will need time for that.

The amazing thing about this signing is how it has sent some newspapers way off on the wrong scent. There have been suggestions that we are ready to sell Gary Stevens because Mel happens to be an international right-back too. Nothing could be further from my mind, though I have had to reassure the player on that one. You wonder how people can add two and two and consistently get seven! Mel is here because of his versatility and because he could be vital for us in the closing stages of the League campaign. It was never a case of playing him or Gary. That didn't form the slightest part of the equation.

Mel will find that he needs a higher level of fitness than he had in the south. All the players coming up here have learned that. Maybe he would not need to have it if he was playing for one of the lesser clubs in the Premier League. Maybe he would not need it if he was at Hamilton or at Motherwell or at Dundee, say, because the challenges which have to be met there are so much less than those we have to meet at Ibrox. Your fitness definitely does have to be that bit higher to play for Rangers.

31 January 1989

At Firhill to take a look at young Tom Cowan, the Clyde left-back. He has been recommended to us and we have been taking a look at him on a reasonably regular basis. In fact, I met John Clark, the Clyde manager, and he told me that the young lad was a great prospect. So Walter has seen him and Phil has been to see him and Gordon Neely, the youth team coach, has been to see him and now it's my turn. Clyde are playing Forfar in a Scottish Cup replay and eventually they lose the tie 1–0 but the lad looks good. He is impressive. The only problem about that is that we are not the only club there who are looking at him. My mate Kenny Dalglish is sitting with me in the directors' box.

Brian Clough's right-hand man at Notts Forest, Ronnie Fenton, is there and the manager of Coventry, John Sillett, is there and ready to do the business that night.

We could not sit back and allow any of them to move in front of us. Right after the game I spoke to John Clark and asked for permission to speak to the boy himself. I arranged to see him the following day with a view to signing him. He had done extremely well and he had only played 16 or 17 games for Clyde in the First Division. He is the kind of young player we are looking for. Big money buys are necessary at our level. But there are other lesser known players, young players whom you have to be ready to take a chance on. We have Davie Kirkwood, bought from East Fife, and we would like to have Tom Cowan as well. Young players like this can grow up in the club and learn in the club alongside the professionals already there. They get the chance to add a soccer education to their natural talents.

1 February 1989

The young lad wants to think things over. I don't blame him for that because Nottingham Forest are in too and they have tempted him. This is a big career move and he wants to make sure it is the right one. We have spelled out to him what is on offer here at Ibrox. We like to think that we can match anyone but when it is a young player and the spell of Cloughie is being woven around him you can only hope that your own words can reach him and convince him.

6 February 1989

Tom Cowan has agreed to join us. I am happy about that because we get a lot of stick about not buying Scottish players when the real facts are that no club is willing to sell to us. You only have to look at the transfer saga which surrounded Richard Gough when he was at Dundee United and they made it plain that they would NEVER under any circumstances sell the player to us.

85

Then we went through all kinds of trouble before finally being able to sign Ian Ferguson from St Mirren. To get him we paid over the odds – but we bought a young player with a bright, bright future and this season he has proved our judgment to be right by forcing his way into the Scotland World Cup squad. But it is not easy to buy players from other clubs in Scotland. Clyde handled the business in a proper manner. We paid them £100,000 and, again, we have a player of real potential. I liked the look of him and so did the rest of the backroom staff. It's possible we have picked a winner.

11 March 1989

It is only five weeks or so since we signed Tom Cowan but he is playing for us today against Hamilton at Ibrox. It is a big jump for the boy. But in training and with the reserves he has served notice that he is ambitious and talented and hungry. I like that hunger about him.

More than 35,000 people see him make his debut – they take to him too. We win 3–0 and he has not been over-awed by his first taste of the Premier League. He looks the kind of lad who wouldn't be overawed by anything at all. Good attitude to have. He has been showing the kind of character that you need to be a Ranger – to get back to that Bill Struth bit. He has a bit of dig about him. So much so that I have had to tell him to ease off in training. Every game is played like a Cup-tie – even a kick-about at the training ground.

12 May 1989

Looking at the signings we have made I think about Tom Cowan and I hope that he will be able to push his way into the first-team. He still has to learn but I think he knows that. In fact, I'm sure he does. He is young, enthusiastic and he wants to impress but any 19-year-old who wants to win as much as he does is going to be a little bit impetuous. He will learn to control that and he

Youngster Tommy Cowan, plucked from Clyde for £100,000, signs on watched by assistant manager Walter Smith.

will be a better player for us when he does. He has a real chance if he applies himself properly.

I remember the day we brought him into the team for the first time against Hamilton. It was because Stuart Munro dropped out during training and we told Tom on the Friday that he would be in the squad for the next day. We told him at lunch-time and there was not the slightest trace of nerves about him. It was not a case of worrying about it – it was a case of looking forward to it. He did fine that day and he did fine when he came in again before the end of the season. But he still has to learn and he still has to work. If he accepts that then I'm looking for him to make it into the squad.

6 June 1989

Perhaps the final piece in the jigsaw is going to fall into place for me. Trevor Steven travelled up to have talks with us at Ibrox. They went well. At least, I think they went well. But there are other clubs who want him. Manchester United would like to sign him. And Everton want to keep him. I don't blame them. He has been an outstanding player for a long, long time. I can remember playing against him when he was still a teenager at Burnley. I have admired him since then and watched his career carefully. In fact, you could say that I have wanted to sign him from the very moment I was appointed as manager here at Ibrox. The chance has never come before now because he was under contract at Goodison. Now that contract has ended, he is a free agent and I hope that I have been able to talk him into joining up with his old Everton team-mate Gary Stevens here at Ibrox. Like most players he wants a challenge and the thought of playing in Europe, particularly in the European Cup, appeals to him.

Trevor is a very fine player and I know that he will add that little bit extra to our team. He won't be looked on as a saviour, as the big star who is going to lead the team back to greatness, which could be the case if he goes to Old Trafford. Here he will be part of a TEAM, a team packed with TALENT, a team we hope is going places and a team which already has success. We came close to winning the treble and we did win two trophies.

An old boy welcomes a new signing – veteran Davie Cooper with Trevor Steven. Cooper has now moved on to play with Motherwell as Steven stakes his own claims for Ibrox stardom.

The target will be retaining the title and he knows that coming here he has the chance of winning medals just as the other lads from England have done. Now I have to wait for his decision. I would like to have it inside 48 hours. I hope I hear positively because I really do look on him as an important signing for this club.

8 June 1989

Good news! We heard this afternoon that Trevor Steven has turned down the offers he received from other clubs and he has decided that he will join us. I have made Everton an offer of one million pounds but they want more and it looks like landing at a tribunal. I would rather that had not happened but he is a player I have wanted for so long that it doesn't matter all that much. The best aspect for all of us at Rangers – apart from the obvious fact that we are getting another international player – is that he has chosen us ahead of several top teams in the south. OK, I may begin to sound boring on the subject, but it underlines once again just how BIG Rangers are.

As far as I am concerned this is the biggest and the best club in Britain and players all across the country are growing to realise that as well. Getting this agreement from Trevor Steven is confirmation for me that Rangers are recognised everywhere as a top team. Not only here in Scotland but right through Britain and on to the continent as well. We won't rest on our laurels after this one. We will continue to look for good players to join our squad but Trevor was a player who was available and a player we wanted. To get him in the face of such strong opposition is a boost for us for the new season. He will join us at the end of this month and be with the rest of the lads when they report for training at the start of July.

30 June 1989

Leeds United have been in touch again about Mel Sterland and this time I have listened to their offer and accepted it. We will get £650,000 and Mel will rejoin his old Sheffield Wednesday boss Howard Wilkinson at Leeds. I spoke to the player about the move, explained the situation to him and he has accepted things.

We had to sign him when we did because we desperately needed cover if any of our defenders was injured on the run in to the League. Or, indeed, if any of them had been suspended for any length of time. He came in, he helped us and he scored a goal or two, but now that we have Trevor Steven there is no room for him in the squad. If you can get a better player then you do that – it has to be that way.

I want the best for Rangers and In my view Trevor will be better for the club than Mel would be. I thanked him for the job he did and for the way he accepted the decision. It was another of those tough decisions managers have to make. I'll always be grateful to Mel for the way he came north and helped us clinch the title. He is a good professional and I am sure that he will do very well with Leeds. I hope so. It would be good to see him win promotion there.

Richard Gough, one of the biggest buys made by Graeme Souness, up against another million pounds plus star, Gary Lineker.

5

Another Skol Cup Victory and a Continuing Scottish Cup Jinx

For all his successes Graeme Souness has found his Cup jinx still haunting him. Last season he thought it might end, instead he was on-field to share another major disappointment in the Scottish Cup.

This time the team did reach the final – but still with a 'treble' beckoning them they slumped to defeat.

It was agony for Souness who failed to win an English cup medal with Liverpool and has failed to win one since joining Rangers. But at least the Skol Cup was there to provide early season success and eventual consolation for the last match failure. It was the third time in succession that Souness and his players had taken the trophy. And it was the second year in succession that Rangers and Aberdeen served up a classic final for the Hampden fans. The tale of two cups is told from the pages of the Souness diary . . .

16 August 1988

One Premier League game played, one victory recorded and now here we are off in defence of the Skol Cup tomorrow night. It doesn't take long in coming around. It has been a good tournament for me since I came to Ibrox. In fact, it couldn't have been better. We won it by beating Celtic in the final in my first season and then there was that classic final at Hampden against Aberdeen last season which we won eventually in a penalty shoot-out. That was a marvellous advertisement for the game and it would be nice to think that we would be back at Hampden this season and that the final would be as exciting and as memorable. And as good for us as the others have been. It has been a competition which has suited us because we seem to have played well at the start of the season. It is a short, sharp knockout tournament which we have enjoyed and which the fans appear to have enjoyed. And, unlike the Scottish Cup, we have not fallen to any sucker punches so far. I only hope I'm not talking too soon here. Tomorrow night we are at Firhill. We have to play Clyde there and I know that John Clark will have his lads well prepared. What we need is for our boys to show the same commitment they did at Hamilton. If they can repeat that then we should be in the next round. Let's hope so... .

17 August 1988

This was an encouraging beginning to our defence of the trophy. We got off to a good start with Kevin Drinkell getting our opening goal after just 17 minutes. That settled the lads and they played well. It was a good playing surface, a nice summer's night and a good crowd. They responded to that and while we had the odd difficult moment – which we had expected playing away from home – we got another goal from Mark Walters before half-time and then one from Derek Ferguson before the end. Not too much to complain about. A solid, professional performance which took us into the next round.

24 August 1988

Skol Cup time again and once more we face First Division opposition, Clydebank – but this time at our own place. And this time the performance is even more professional than it was last week. We have more than 34,000 people at the game and they see six goals go crashing in. The nice thing about this, too, is that the goals are shared all around the team. Ally McCoist started if off, Richard Gough joined in and then we had the others coming from Mark Walters, Ray Wilkins, Kevin Drinkell and Ian Durrant. We were never under any pressure and even though we all realise that to win a tournament for the third year in succession is a tall order, we have to believe we will be in there somewhere at the death after the way we have kicked off the season. Only three more games to go in this one if we reach the final – and just 50 or so more in the other competitions.

31 August 1988

Only one team from outside the Premier League is involved at this stage now – Dunfermline. All you can hope for in any tournament when it comes to it is for a home draw. We got that and we also drew Dundee. This time we got off to a quick start when McCoist put away a 15th minute penalty and then Mark Walters scored and one of their defenders put one past his own keeper right on half-time. That saw us three goals ahead at the interval and we were then left coasting towards the semi-finals in the second half. They did score eight minutes from the end when Stuart Rafferty grabbed a goal for them but our lads simply stepped up a gear once more and Ian Ferguson scored our fourth two minutes later. That was us in the last four and this time just under 40,000 fans had been in the ground to see us do it. There were interesting results in the other games tonight too. Dundee United defeated Celtic at Tannadice, Hearts knocked out Dunfermline with a 4–1 win at East End Park – good going that – and Aberdeen won at Easter Road. That was also an impressive victory and the game had to go to extra-time before the two teams were separated. The possibility of a repeat of last year's final is still on, then. We'll see... .

20 September 1988

Aberdeen beat Dundee United at Dens Park tonight in the first of the two semi-finals. Now we have to face Hearts tomorrow and if we do win then the action replay of last year's Hampden clash will be on. That's what everyone seems to want – except for Hearts and their fans, of course.

We beat Hearts on Saturday at Tynecastle when Ian Durrant scored with a penalty and Scott Nisbett snatched a second before big Terry scored an own goal. It should have given us a bit of confidence but we had to go into that game without McCoist and then Drinkell was injured and the strike force we looked for so much from won't make it for the Hampden semi tomorrow. So if the win gave *us* a boost then the team sheets when they are exchanged will give *them* a lift!

21 September 1988

It is not the side we would want to be playing and, like Saturday, I have had to put myself on the bench again along with Andy Gray whom we have brought back home to give us cover in the present emergency. That's a fair age total on that bench – but Andy and I try not to think about that! We both go on during the game but thankfully Mark Walters had one of these magical nights he is always capable of. He took them on by himself. He scored one goal early and one goal late and in between young Scott Nisbett helped himself to another. We are back in the final in spite of the team problems we have had to overcome. A huge crowd of 53,623 saw us do it and they were privileged to see Mark play in this way. It was a memorable performance from him. He is just so skilful and tonight the poor Hearts' defenders could do nothing to stop him. I doubt if anyone could have, the mood he was in.

We are playing really well just now. The grounds are good, the players are eager to get to the games after their pre-season training in Tuscany and apart from the hiccups over the striking positions, we are fielding a strong, strong team. You don't like looking too far ahead at any time in this business but when we are on song then it will take a very, very good performance from a very, very good team to stop us. I believe that... .

22 September 1988

Nice to look back and realise that we won convincingly without our main strikers and nice to relish that display from Mark

Gary Stevens – Souness reckons him the best defender in Britain – rises to clear a Hearts' attack as Richard Gough watches and waits.

Walters. I don't think there is any extra pressure on the players because this is their third final in succession in this Skol Cup.

Players should feel some kind of pressure all the time. In every game, really. They have to feel that because they have to want to do well all the time, for the team, for themselves, for their families. You don't necessarily need any extra pressure – just the type of thing you live with all through any season. I like to think that the professionals I have gathered around me are the type of players who welcome the pressure of being expected to win every game. They can handle that – or they should be able to handle it. That is why I bought them in the first place! I looked at each one of them and decided that he would be able to perform at his highest capabilities with Rangers no matter what was stacked against him. That is the way it is going so far and when we get down to the wire we will see if any of them crack. My money is on them because most of them are battle-hardened pro's.

15 October 1988

Day off because of the World Cup next week and the planning is spot on for that but I have to wonder sometimes about the way other fixtures are arranged. Next weekend we are playing the Skol Cup final on the Sunday at Hampden against Aberdeen. It is the first show-piece of the season. It could go to extra-time as it did last year. It will be totally demanding and yet we are in Europe just 72 hours later playing a UEFA Cup-tie in West Germany against Cologne. Walter has been to see Cologne. He saw them in midweek when we won at Easter Road and I will have to go to see them again next Saturday, just before the Aberdeen match.

We are in Europe trying to do our best for ourselves, yes, but also for Scotland. The European ties are set years in advance, the League must recognise by this time that the Skol Cup will be contested nine years out of ten by teams who are in Europe and yet there it is, scheduled just before a European tie. And on a Sunday – while Cologne are insisting that we play there on Wednesday. Recovery time will be nil. Surely someone in authority will try to make sure that this does not happen next season? I would like to think so. Still, we cannot dwell on it too much and we cannot let it affect the players. That is the last thing we want. We have enough problems over the Skol final after Ian Durrant's injury to worry us. We don't need any more. Not a single one!

21 October 1988

Two days to go to the final and the countdown is on – even though we also have to think about Cologne. I have to interrupt my own preparations for Hampden by flying to Germany to see Cologne in action against Werder Bremen, coincidentally the team Celtic will play in their European Cup second round game. It is a nuisance but it has to be done. You have to be able to take a look at European opposition as often as you can. We cannot turn our backs on seeing them again in this one.

That is just a minor irritation, really. The worrying thing about the game on Sunday is the way it seems to have been hyped up into a 'grudge game' in the press. That is the last thing we need and the last thing we want. I think we are all conscious enough about the feelings over Ian Durrant's injury without it being mentioned as often as it has been. We don't want anyone in our team going out to Hampden and looking for revenge. We don't want any involvement in that way. All we want is to go out to play a game of football. No matter how important the game is, there seems a danger of the final itself being overshadowed by the events at Pittodrie two weeks ago. It would be a tragedy if that were to happen on the day. And, just now, that is very much on my mind. It is a nagging worry and I know already that I will have to speak to the players about it before the final.

This must sound simple to anyone outside the game. But it isn't. What I will have to do is warn the players who are taking part in the final that I don't want to see them involved in any trouble, I have to try to get them to curb their tempers and I have to do that in such a way that their normal attitude is not altered. We cannot afford to kill their natural instincts. I have players who are winners. They have still to retain that edge even though I may have to warn them to walk away from any confrontations. There is a knife edge situation here. Go too far down one road and you finish up knocking all the fight out of the players. Don't go down the road at all and you could end up with the first show-piece of the season being scarred by vendettas. It's something to think about while I'm travelling to West Germany. And just something else to worry about, as well!

A cup final should not be played in the shadow of other events. It should stand on its own and be allowed to stand on its own with it own very special importance to the season. None of us will forget Durrant and the injury he has but the best way of showing him how we feel about him is by winning the Cup. I have to get that over to them. It is essential.

23 October 1988

Before the game began I sat the players down in the dressing-room knowing what I was going to say to them. The whole problem has been eating away at me. I had to make sure there were no personal vendettas. This was not the stage for revenge – this was the stage for another football classic. I had to get that over to them. I told them that we would not tolerate anyone getting involved. I told them that the greatest favour we could do Ian Durrant was lifting the Cup for the third year in succession. I told them that we had to make sure that this was a game to match the one everyone had saluted last year. And I warned them that if anyone did get involved in any kind of revenge action then they would be letting down themselves, the Rangers Football Club and Ian Durrant.

I was genuinely worried about the match because of the glare of publicity which had surrounded the possibility of grudges being settled. And, also, because Durrant was one of the most popular players in the dressing-room. Everyone had been upset about the injury. Everyone had been genuinely worried about him and about how he would cope with the operation and the recovery period. I was thinking about that all the time, knowing that there could be a flashpoint – as there can be in any game at all – but recognising, always, as far as this one is concerned that the least little bit of trouble will be blown up into a major incident. We have players with a bit of temperament – as Aberdeen do. And so naturally that is there gnawing away at me. Now, looking back at the way the lads approached things I have nothing but admiration for them. It was a test of their temperament. A test of their character – and they passed the test. Eventually it was a final which rivalled the last one and this time we did not need a penalty shoot-out to take the trophy.

Goals from Ally McCoist and Ian Ferguson were cancelled out in each half by Davie Dodds of Aberdeen. But Dodds could not cancel out the last one, the winner which came from Coisty again with only two minutes left. So we could celebrate and we could look back on a game which had been fraught with danger but which never developed into the brawl some had predicted. We made sure that Durrant had a medal and we all felt that this had been a game the players had won for him. I'm sure the majority of the supporters in the massive 72,122 crowd on that Sunday afternoon at Hampden spared a thought for him too. He might not have played but his presence was out there with the lads.

That Sunday, for me, was also the day Ian Ferguson was finally accepted by the fans. The season before, after we had bought him from St Mirren, he had shuttled back and forward between the midfield and the front because of the problems we had at that time. Then when the season started he was out after picking up a knock in the Davie Cooper Testimonial Match against Bordeaux. He did not play in the first few games and then at Hampden he scored a spectacular goal in the second half and he played well throughout. I went to him at the end because I was so pleased that the crowd had eventually been won over by him. It had seemed to me for so long that they had not appreciated his worth to the team. That goal helped prove to them just how important a player he will be for Rangers. How important he has already BEEN for Rangers. He will be at this club for a long, long time and he will be a Scotland player soon. There is no doubt in my mind about that. And, thankfully, a lot of other doubts have been dispelled this afternoon. It's amazing what a goal can do... .

As for the result itself, well, here we are with a trophy tucked away already. The season is just three months old and the first cup is back in the Ibrox Trophy Room. It's important in several ways. Important in its own right as one of the major honours of the season. Important because it means that we have qualified for Europe this early in the season – at the very least we will be back in the UEFA Cup next year. Important, too, because it maintains our record in the tournament since I became manager. That's now three years in the Skol Cup without losing a game. It's a nice little record to have. And important, too, because it has served notice on the rest of the teams in the country that we have overcome the difficulties of last season and that we are in there challenging for every honour this season. The gauntlet is down. We mean business and we are all hoping that the Skol Cup win is just the beginning.

28 January 1989

Still at the top of the Premier League despite having injury problems which persist – particularly those affecting Ian Durrant, Chris Woods and Ally McCoist. Key players, all internationals and all missing at a crucial period of the season. Now it's time to think about the Scottish Cup and I don't know if it is something I want to think about. You get superstitious in this funny old game and I am no exception. The one which haunts me every year around this time is the Cup jinx which has followed me through my years at Anfield and on to the years I have had with Rangers. It's incredible but I can't rid myself of the feeling that I am destined never to know success in the Cup. I can only hope that the jinx will apply to me only as a player – I couldn't bear the thought of jinxing Rangers for the rest of my time here as a manager. The only time I have been able to beat it was when I was with Sampdoria in Italy and we won the Italian Cup. At Liverpool we never had a sniff in my time – it was only after I had left that Kenny managed to get himself a medal at Wembley in the FA Cup. And now here I am looking at a troublesome tie tomorrow at Kirkcaldy and wondering if I will have to put myself on the bench, knowing I probably will have to do that and fearing the worst because of it.

God, don't I have enough worries over the injuries without having to take this Cup jinx on board again for another season? It's a dreadful thought – for me to be there on the bench and maybe watch the team go out. Our record so far is dreadful. If

Ian Ferguson, at last accepted by the fans, says Graeme Souness who is also in this picture from Premier League action.

the Skol Cup has handed me some very pleasing moments, the Scottish Cup has given me the biggest boots in the backside that the game has been able to offer me in Scotland so far!

The first season saw a defeat from Hamilton at Ibrox in a result which stunned the whole country. I should have known better than to expect anything else. The next season we hobbled through against Raith Rovers only after a replay at our own place after we had failed to win at Starks Park. Then, with that game out of the way we went back to Fife, to Dunfermline this time, and out we went again. Twice we lost to teams who were later relegated from the Premier League. It is hard to believe unless you take my Cup pedigree or lack of it into account.

Now it's a return to Starks Park and we know it is going to be a sell out there and we have even more injury problems – hence the dilemma I find myself in. We will see how things are in the morning.

29 January 1989

Neale Cooper is not right. We can't take a chance with him and so the other gamble we have to take is to put me on the bench as one of the substitutes. Ally McCoist will be on the bench with me as he tries to get himself match fit, but this is the bottom of the barrel for us. Jimmy Nicholl is in the team and I am a reserve and we just don't have anyone else available.

Watching the game, I was thinking to myself, "Here we go again." I asked myself what I was doing sitting out there on the bench and it hit me worst of all when they scored after half-time. Gordon Dalziel got the goal and they deserved it – but that was no consolation at all for me right then when that ball went into the net. Quarter of an hour later Ian Ferguson equalised. It was a stunning goal; a shot which I scarcely saw because he hit it so hard and so accurately. That saved the match for us and saved me from potential suicide!

The time between the goals wasn't much but in that 15 minutes or so I saw all the Cup disappointments I had had – and there have been many – flash back in my mind. It was a terrible time and I was blaming myself and also promising myself that I would not get involved in the Scottish Cup ever again. This was to be the last time. Fergie's goal gave us a lifebelt and also allowed Raith the chance to return to Ibrox in a replay for the second year in succession. A nice consolation prize for them with a big gate certain – but just a lucky escape for me. I could not look on that result as anything else. It was agony for me.

1 February 1989

Frank Connor brings his team to Ibrox and an astonishing crowd of more than 40,000 turn out to see how we handle this second clash. We handle it so much better than we had the first one – probably because I am not involved in a playing sense. I'm glad that we have players who are available again. I could not have gone through a second bout of worrying over my jinx.

Gough is in again, so is Neale Cooper and Coisty is fit enough to play from the start. That helps us enormously and we are helped still more when Mark Walters scores the opening goal in the 34th minute. When Kevin Drinkell gets a second two minutes into the second half the party is over for the Rovers. Before the end Cammy Fraser puts through his own goal and we win 3–0 and are rewarded with a home tie against Stranraer. It looks easy. Simple, in fact. But so did Hamilton and so did Raith Rovers and Dunfermline and all the time we were being left with egg on our faces. I'm saying nothing about this one coming up later this month. Except that I have made up my mind that come what may I will not be stripped for it. No way!

18 September 1989

Little Stranraer are the second of the smaller clubs to benefit from a Cup day at Ibrox. This time the gate is even higher than it was against the Rovers. We attract 41,198 – far and away the biggest attendance in Scotland that day. This time there are no hiccups, no hitches and never the slightest chance of a shock. The players go out to do the job they have been asked to do. Woodsy is back in goal and that's a good omen! Again I am not stripped to play – and that's another good omen! We score eight goals and these are shared between five players. John Brown gets two. So do Kevin Drinkell and Ally McCoist. The others come from Ian Ferguson and Mark Walters and suddenly we have gone further in the Scottish Cup than we have ever done since I became manager. It's a nice feeling even though I still see my main contribution as being the very negative one of staying off the pitch.

It was a good performance but it was without any doubt a marvellous crowd. I know the Cup is always that little bit special but to see gates almost shut for a game against Stranraer is something else. I don't think even in my best days at Liverpool, we would have been able to tempt that many people at Anfield for a tie which is not among the more glamorous available. It is a tribute to our support. Fantastic – and for me it is a support which is still growing and growing. The better we get then the bigger the support will get. I don't doubt that for a moment.

21 March 1989

Any Scottish Cup appears to turn into a tough test for us but this time in the quarter-final tie it IS hard. We have Dundee United, but we had to wait a little time before finding out who our opponents were to be. It took two replays to prise apart United and their rivals in the north-east, Aberdeen. The first match at Pittodrie was a 1–1 draw and the first replay at Tannadice finished the same way with both the goals arriving in extra-time. Then in the third Mixu Paatelainen who had scored in the two previous games struck again with a late goal which sent Aberdeen toppling from the tournament and left United to travel to us today.

United are a problem team because they are the kind of side who play equally well away from home as they do at home. Having them at Ibrox is exactly the same as playing them at Tannadice in my book. There is no home advantage and no disadvantage where they are concerned. They are also the only team to have beaten us at Ibrox this season so far when Dave Beaumont scored a late goal for them back before Christmas. It would be nice to get a taste of revenge for the defeat – but equally it would just be nice to win again and get another step along the road to Hampden and Cup final day.

Unfortunately it's a day when we hit rock bottom in a shocking first-half performance. We are dreadful and they are leading by a goal from Kevin Gallacher when we go in at half-time. He scored in 18 minutes and for all our huffing and puffing we have not looked like cancelling that one out. It is a bad day – but in the second half we change it all around. Within 35 minutes Kevin Drinkell and Ally McCoist have both snatched goals and we are in front. Unhappily for us the big Finnish international striker Paatelainen has not lost his Cup goal touch. He grabs an equaliser with only ten minutes remaining and so we have to head up to Tannadice in midweek. We had so many chances to win the game but we didn't take them and Ally McCoist missed so many of them. Normally if you want chances to fall to any player then you hope they will fall to him. This time they did but he couldn't take them. He got one out of six and all that did was keep us in the Cup when just one more of all those other goal chances could have carried us into the last four.

27 March 1989

We beat Hibs at home on Saturday and Coisty scored, so maybe he is getting in the mood for tonight. We simply cannot afford to miss chances again the way they were missed last week. That would be disastrous. It could put us out of the tournament and I know that Coisty realises this. In the dressing-room before this game there is a bit of banter going and Ally has been told that the journey wouldn't really have been necessary but for him. So, never short of an answer, he has told the lads that he'll sort it out. What's more, he does it. A goal five minutes after half-time is all that is needed and Coisty is as good as his word. He gets it, and it takes us into a semi-final against St Johnstone. Our Old Firm rivals Celtic are also in the last four and they have to face Hibs as the whole country looks for an Old Firm final. Who knows? Maybe this time... .

15 April 1989

Semi-final day at Parkhead against the men from the First Division, St Johnstone. Alex Totten, who was assistant manager with Rangers before I came to the club, has worked hard to get his team into this glamour game. We know that they are well-organised. We know that this is their big day and we have spent our time impressing on the players that only their best will get them through. So many people have us in the final already that it's a worry. We have spent the last week concerned that this will affect the players. After ten minutes or so we realise that it has and the warnings we were trying so hard to hammer home to them have been forgotten. This turns out to be one of our poorest performances as far as attitude is concerned. They just are not right from the start. You warn them and you warn them and you warn them and they go out and they think that they will be able to go through by only putting in 75 or 80 per cent effort. And St Johnstone, well, they were up for this one. They were on a high, they were giving more than 100 per cent and so we were caught out. We never looked like losing the game – but nor did we look like winning it. And we did not deserve to win it either. This turned out to be a game to forget ... and now we have the thought of another replay in front of us.

18 April 1989

Celtic have beaten Hibs 3–1 in their Sunday semi at Hampden. Now the country waits for us to see if an Old Firm final is going to be played this year. We know it should be – but we could not do the job on Saturday. Now we have to make no mistakes tonight. Incredibly, our fans are still there, still turning out in huge numbers in spite of the disappointment they must all have felt at the weekend. Although it is a Tuesday night there are still 44,205 in Celtic Park – and that is only 3,000 less than the Saturday gate. It never ceases to amaze me how the fans dig deep into their pockets to support this team. They are an amazing bunch of people – and I just want our lads to go out there and give them the result they deserve.

Within five minutes of the start of the game I knew they were going to be OK. This time they were on the ball from the kick-off and I think they reacted to the criticism they had received from the fans and from the media. I did throw in a few words myself!

I was less than happy at the way they had approached the first game and I let them know that in no uncertain terms, mainly because it seemed that they hadn't listened to anything we had told them. We had tried to stress to them that no matter how good you are in relation to the opposition if you go into a game with the wrong attitude then you will slip up. There is no doubt about that. But we had a good night in this replay and the goals from Mark Walters, Gary Stevens, Kevin Drinkell and Ally McCoist saw us crash through to the final against Celtic.

That will be a sell out. We know that and we know that our fans will roll up to back us yet again, just as they have done right through this competition. Our two games away from home at Starks Park and at Tannadice were sell outs and every other game we played topped the 40,000 mark. It shows incredible faith and, as I said, I am just happy that the players gave these fans the result they deserved tonight – and allied the result to a performance which was also what the supporters deserved to see. I think the way the fans turned out for these games reflects their feelings for the club and I want all my players to realise that. They have to take that on board to recognise just what this club means to so many thousands and thousands of people. It really does make you feel humble when you see guys spending money on replays when that money might be going to their families. All you want to do is repay them with results. There is no doubt that is what they deserve because they never cease to surprise me. No matter where we go, the supporters will be there with us at whatever cost.

12 May 1989

I'm looking towards our first Scottish Cup final since Walter Smith and I took over here. It is an exciting prospect but suddenly we have injury worries that we could have done without. We have coped with injuries all the way through the season but they tended to be scattered around the side. Now, this week of all weeks, they have hit us in midfield. All of them are there and it is a vital area for us. We want to control things there because that is where the game will probably be decided. But, now, as well as the loss of Ian Durrant which we have had to cope with since October, we have three more injury blows. Ray Wilkins who has had such a good season is very doubtful. So is Derek Ferguson whose shoulder injury keeps returning to bother him. He is going in for a close season operation and it is a worry for us thinking about pushing him into such an important match. And we also have Neale Cooper in hospital facing an operation this week.

Add these problems to the sloppiness which the team showed in the League game against Aberdeen at Ibrox and you can understand how worrying this week has become. The game against Aberdeen annoyed me. It did not matter that the League had been won. It did not matter that the game meant nothing in terms of winning or losing the title. Pride should have entered into it. Professionalism should have taken us to another victory to allow the fans another little celebration. The time to relax is only when all the games are over and I have told the players that. They have to remember that Celtic have won nothing so far this season and they will be a hungry team at Hampden. They took the double last season and they won't like the thought of Rangers taking the treble this time round. They will be all out to stop us. Everyone at Ibrox has to realise that. We may have won the Skol Cup and the championship. But these are past, over and done with. It's this weekend which will decide if my own personal cup jinx is ever going to end.

13 May 1989

I have told the newspapers today that Ray Wilkins will not play in the final – but the news inside Ibrox has been worse even than that. We had to decide today that Derek Ferguson would not play in the game either. It was a tremendously difficult decision for us to have to take but we could not see any way round it. The boy was desperate to play in the game. He was so keen to be in the final and so keen to help us out of our injury problems. But it was too big a risk for us to take. It would only take a knock on that damaged shoulder in the first ten minutes to have Fergie

Derek Ferguson celebrates a Player of the Year award with Davie Cooper, Ian Ferguson, Stuart Munro and Davie Kirkwood.

sidelined and we would have looked so foolish. It was a gamble we simply could not afford to take. Everyone knows the problem he has – a knock in a game which is always known for being physical would be enough to have us at a disadvantage and to have Fergie out of action.

Although I have not played first-team football for months there is little alternative but to get myself organised to take a place on the bench. It is not an ideal situation but there are few alternatives left to us now. When it comes to Cup finals all managerial decisions are hard. Tomorrow I will have to tell three players they are not taking part – Derek Ferguson, Andy Gray and Ian McCall who might have come into the frame because of the injury position we find ourselves in. I suppose some people will snipe that we have spent a lot of money and still find ourselves struggling to get a team on the field for a vital Cup final. But I defy any team in the country to have themselves so well covered that FOUR midfield injuries would not affect them, especially as three of the players involved are international class – Wilkins, Durrant and Ferguson. You try to have decent enough cover but in some cases it is impossible to be that well organised. I know that right at this moment.

When I think of the injury problems we have already surmounted on the way to two trophies it seems particularly hard to have to suffer like this for our first final. But we cannot allow any hint of despair to reach the players. We have to get on with the job tomorrow and still try to take the trophy. It is, if you like, just another challenge and these players have been facing them all season. What's new?

14 May 1989

Before the game I had to tell Fergie that he was out. It was a difficult decision and I had to say to him that we would be back next year to get him a medal. But I didn't find it as hard as I thought I might because it is a part of the job. My job as manager is to do my best to make Rangers Football Club successful and if you have to take on board difficult jobs then that is it. They have to be done and if you believe you are right then the breaking of bad news to someone isn't as hard as people might think.

Clash of two men who used to face each other in the English First Division – Rangers' striker Kevin Drinkell and former Celtic centre-half Mick McCarthy.

I always feel that if I was on the receiving end of bad news from a manager then I would be out to prove him wrong. I remember Tottenham sold me because they didn't think I was good enough for the English First Division. I was a kid then, 19 years old, I think I was, and all I had in mind when I went to Middlesbrough was that I would prove them wrong. I like to think I did that. Any player I allow to leave Ibrox or any player I leave out of the team should take the same attitude. It is the only one to have. But, in Fergie's case, I think he might have been just a little bit relieved as well as disappointed at missing out on a Hampden final. He knew deep down that the injury could wreck things for him and for the team. It was the only decision to make.

I only hope that the players don't think I am naming myself just to try to get a medal because I missed one with Liverpool and have not had a chance here in Scotland to get a Cup win. That is furthest from my mind. We have talked about it and there doesn't seem to be any other choice to make.

In the end, right or wrong, it does not affect the outcome of the game. A mix up between the linesman and the referee allows Celtic to take a throw in over on the right and then a mistake by Gary Stevens allows Joe Miller to score. That one moment, these two mistakes, cost us the Cup.

It was not a good game. We did not play well. I don't think they played particularly well either – but the break that was going went their way. We thought we had a good goal disallowed and Ally McCoist cannot be happy with the chance he missed. It should have been a goal. Earlier in the season when he was scoring so regularly it would have been a goal. But, in a way, I was happy with some parts of our game. We were winning the 50–50 balls, we were battling well in a game which was always going to be physical. And we proved that we were as hungry as Celtic.

I felt so sorry for Gary Stevens because he was the best player on the field that day. OK, he made a mistake but he did not hide after it. He still looked for the ball, he was never marked absent. He did not allow that mistake to affect him and that taught me something about him. That is what I want from my players, from all of them. I don't want to see them hiding after a mistake. I want to see them keep on performing professionally. It is the only way. Our fans are very demanding – and they have every right to be – and the players have to be ready to face up to them after making mistakes. Gary did. And on the biggest day of the season. That impressed me. I spoke to him briefly afterwards but he knew – he is professional enough to know when a mistake has been made.

After that game I thanked all the players for a wonderful season. I did not want a Cup final defeat, especially one which happened in the circumstances which surrounded this one, to take anything away from what they had achieved earlier in the season. There are two trophies at Ibrox including the most important one of all – the League Championship trophy! And I hope I am thanking them in the same way at the end of next season. They all deserved my thanks and the thanks of everyone who supports Rangers. I was sorry the final had not been a classic game. Sorrier that we could not give the fans a treble to celebrate, but one day and one defeat could not take away the good days and the good results which had happened all the way through the season.

6

Injuries – And A Tragic Blow For Ian Durrant

The cruellest blow Rangers suffered last season was the injury to Ian Durrant, the midfield player Souness knew was destined for the top. He was already a key World Cup player for his country and a youngster whose importance to Rangers was growing with every game. At Aberdeen in October 1988 he was injured and he has not played again. Souness suffered with him as you can read here; just as he worried over the mystery virus which saw Chris Woods miss a large slice of the season. Both were blows which could have cost the Ibrox club the title they wanted. Yet, somehow, the other players shrugged them off and got on with the job of winning. But all of them were thinking of Ian Durrant when they won the first trophy of the season, the Skol Cup. And his slim shadow hung over the celebrations as the championship race ended with Durrant still a reluctant spectator after undergoing a second operation on his damaged knee.

12 August 1988

The eve of another new season. Like everyone else we start off with high hopes and, looking at the squad and looking at the preparations, I think we have got things right pre-season. The buys should be OK and the training seemed ideal. The lads all worked hard and they played a couple of games over there before coming back for the more serious matches. Nothing too big, this time, though. Just a build up towards the opening Premier League match. The only worry on the horizon is the constant fear of injuries to key players. Last season was a nightmare for us. And, since I came here as manager, I have found it hard to come to terms with the amount of injuries we pick up.

At Liverpool we did not collect as many. One season we took the title using only FOURTEEN players. And that was not exceptional. You did not seem to be burdened to the same extent with knocks, serious or otherwise. I have a theory about this. When teams play against us then it's a cup final for them. They want to beat us. They want to do so well against us that they are all trying like bears to cause an upset. So, if you look at Motherwell then their games against Rangers are FOUR finals for them. And Celtic find the same thing. The Old Firm players have to face 40 or more Cup finals every season – because every game they play is the same. Fiercely competitive with tremendous physical demands made on the players. Every time we face any team in the country they are up and they are bombing and their commitment is so much greater than it will be in a game against a team in the middle of the table or at the foot of the table. So our players have to be ready for that. In answer to that our players have to say, "No, this is not for me", or they have to stand up to the challenge week after week after week. There are no rest days. No time to have off days. And so the mental and physical stress the Old Firm players are under is immense. And I don't see that lessening.

The pressures have always been there but the Premier League where you face each other four times a season, at least, has increased the tension for all the players with the Big Two. There is a greater stress factor on a player at Ibrox than there is on a player at, say, Liverpool. And I can say that because I have been at both places.

It brings to mind a story told to me about Bill Struth, the legendary Rangers' manager, who ran the club for so long and who pushed the club into its pre-eminent position in Scottish soccer. It was the sports writer Jim Rodger – a man who is respected more than anyone else in his business – who told me this one. Apparently Struth used to say to players he was intending to sign: "I hear you are a great player, son, but can you play for the Rangers?" And that is what it's all about.

At Liverpool we used to know when we had a few easy games coming up, a few where you knew that you would be taking two points no matter what happened. That isn't the case here. I tell players when they sign that they have to be ready for this challenge because they are coming to somewhere unique. Someplace which is really like no other. The Struth words which were probably first uttered more than 50 years ago still apply, perhaps even more now than in his day. These words rattle around my head. They echo in my mind every time I see a player I know can do better start to struggle in a game which should be easy for him. But none of them are easy. None of them can be taken lightly. What Bill Struth was saying, in effect, is what I tell the players today: "When you cross that line and go out on to the pitch then you had better be ready."

At the level we are operating now you have to have players with a totally professional approach all the time. It is no use having a player going out on to the pitch not fancying it because it's maybe Douglas Park on a bitterly cold winter's day. Or, maybe not fancying it because they have had a row with their girlfriend or their wife. They have to be thinking only about the game, only about going out there and doing the business. Going out there and winning! It can't be any other way. Not now. Not in these highly competitive days. And you need nine or ten players operating at that level every week if you are to win the games you have to win to be champions. Maybe 30 years ago you could do it with four or five operating at top form every week. Maybe in Jim Baxter's era you could manage it with half-a-dozen hitting their best form in each game. Now you need more because the demands are much greater. And, correspondingly, the rewards are so much higher. I'm saying ten players now – soon it will be eleven if that day has not already arrived. At Ibrox no one can relax. Not a single one of us. And that's the way it should be at the top.

119

8 October 1988

We lost our first Premier League game today – at Aberdeen. But the result does not matter to any of us. All we can think about going back on the team bus is the injury suffered by Ian Durrant. I think the journey down was a nightmare for us all, but, obviously it was even worse for Durrant. He is the one who is injured. He is the one who faces a knee operation. He is the one who will be out for a long, long time. It is heartbreaking for him and heartbreaking for us all.

The fact that the game is lost is insignificant. Tonight our dreams of the title were pushed into the background. The worry is over a young player who has the world at his feet. He is the best player of his type in British football. He is the perfect mobile midfield player who gets forward and gets himself into the opposing penalty box and causes havoc there because it is impossible to mark that kind of player. He has an instinctive knack of pushing himself into the danger areas and he is the near-perfect modern-day midfielder.

There are only a couple of players I have played with or against in my time who remind me of him. One is Colin Bell who played for Manchester City and England and then there was Terry McDermott of Liverpool whom I played with for a long, long time. They each seemed able to get stronger and stronger as the game went on. Durrant has been the same for us. I remember Durrant in the Skol Cup final in my first season here as manager. The game went into extra time and it was almost as if he said to himself, 'It's time to go into another gear now.' He did just that and start running away from people. It is frightening the reserves of energy and stamina that he possesses.

The doctor has told us that the injury is serious. It looks as if he will be out for the rest of the season and it will be tomorrow after the specialist sees him that we will get further news. I only hope it is better news that we all expect tonight... .

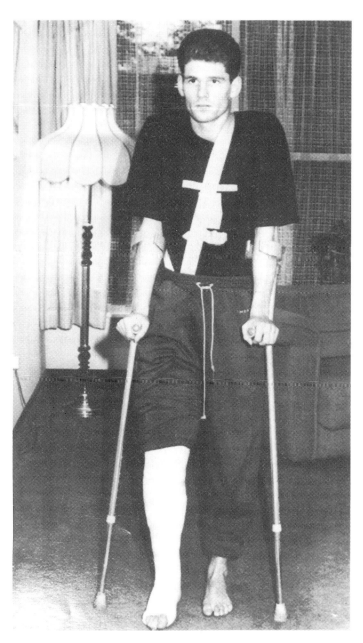

*Injury victim Ian Durrant as he recovers from his first operation
on the damaged knee ligaments which threatened his career.*

9 October 1988

Durrant went through an operation today in a private nursing home. Originally the surgeon was to wait until tomorrow but when he realised the extent of the damage to the knee he made up his mind to carry out the surgery required straight away. It is bad. It is as bad as the doc feared at Pittodrie and it is hard to accept that a young player's footballing future is in doubt because of one bad tackle. It happens in the game. We all know it happens but when it happens so close to home then you feel it really badly.

At the start of the season if anyone had come to me and said that I was going to lose one of my players with a serious injury, with a career-threatening injury, then Ian Durrant would have been the last one, the very last one I would have wanted this to happen to. Firstly, because of his outstanding ability – potentially there is no limit to what he might achieve in the game. Secondly, because with his fitness he could play for the next 15 years at the top if he looks after himself. And thirdly, he was the biggest asset to Rangers Football Club in playing terms. He was the last player I would have wanted this to happen to.

I had had two years working with the boy and trying to point him in the right direction. I had had rows with him. I argued with him. I had his parents up to talk to them. We fell out and sometimes the rows were spectacularly public – and it was because I knew the boy had a unique talent and I did not want to see him waste that. After all that I suddenly felt that we were getting through to him. His attitude at the start of this season was right. It was begining to drop into place and that is how it was when this happened.

I don't feel able to put into words just how badly I feel. It is shattering. And, really, he is a player that this should not have happened to. He didn't deserve to pick up this kind of injury. I would never have believed that he could be so severely injured because he was so bright out there on the field. He had a kind of built-in radar which sensed trouble coming and gave him time to get out of the way of heavy tackles. I did not think that anyone could hurt him. I just thought that Durrant was going to be there for the rest of this season and the next season and the one after that. He is one of the kids you build the future of this club around. Now we won't have him again this season and we have to accept for the moment that there are question marks over his long-term future.

I hope that is wrong. I just want to see him back. I want to see him out there playing again. I think it has hit me badly because my instant reaction had been that it could not be serious. I thought maybe he would have a gash on his leg. I was sure that it was a cut. I did not really think that anyone would be able to kick him simply because he was always so cute at avoiding trouble on the field. When I went in at half-time Durrant wasn't the priority for me because as far as I was concerned he just didn't get injured. But on this occasion there seemed to be something about the timing of the tackle which caught him out. He had not expected it and therefore he was caught and his knee was damaged and his career is now in danger.

Why could it not have happened to me? Why could it not be me in that hospital? I am not trying to be Billy big about this – but here I am ending my career. It would have been better to happen to me. Not to a kid who is starting out. And not to a kid who has never hurt anyone in his life. The type of player I have been, maybe it should have happened to me. I have given out a few knocks and I have taken a few knocks myself – so maybe this was one I could have taken. I might even have thought it was a balancing up of the books. Who knows, maybe I would have deserved it! But not him. Not Ian Durrant.

We have players who live by the sword, just as other clubs have the same kind of players. Guys who relish the physical side of the game, the challenge that part of the game represents. But it should not have happened to a youngster who was such a pure footballer. All he had in his body was football, all he wanted to do was play the game – he would not have known how to stop anyone else playing. His game was to go out and entertain.

It should not have happened to him. It really shouldn't! It is a genuine tragedy. For the boy. And for the game as a whole. Whoever brought him to this club must have been so proud to see the way he has developed. And I like to think that I was able to help him along the way. I was patting myself on the back since the season started because he had made the effort to channel all his energies into the game. I could see the change in him. He was so much more responsible – then this has to happen.

10 October 1988

I have been to see Ian Durrant and he is being very brave about everything – which is what you would expect from him. But the surgeon told me that the knee was going to have to be almost totally rebuilt. He said that he had never seen an injury as bad, except maybe when someone had been in a serious car crash. It was the worst sporting injury he had seen. The whole joint of the knee had separated. But with all the marvels of medicine now available we hope against hope that he will be OK. Certainly if anyone can come back from this type of injury then it's him. He may not look strong but he is. He is wiry and he is tougher than you would imagine. He has a mental toughness about him too.

14 November 1988

Still suffering a little from the Parkhead defeat and now we have news that Chris Woods is ill. There is a midweek game coming against Hamilton and he won't make that. Even more worrying though is the fact that no one seems to know what's wrong with the lad. He has been feeling dizzy and his vision is blurred and he isn't able to do any training just now. I wish I had never thought about or talked about injuries at the start of the season. I thought that we were going to be clear this year after the nightmares we had to suffer last season but it looks like a re-run of all the horrors we went through before. We had Ian Durrant and right now we are without Ally McCoist though at least his injury is something we can look at and treat even if it might take longer than we want. The Durrant injury and now this blow to Woodsy are different. We don't have the slightest idea when we will be able to have them back in the side and that is a major problem.

Mind you, it's an even bigger problem for the boys themselves. They don't know either when they will be ready to play and I can imagine what is going through their minds. It's hellish!

Part of the attraction of Rangers to English stars has been the history of success which has surrounded the club down through its history. Here Chris Woods gets a glimpse of that history in the Trophy Room.

30 November 1988

Still no further forward with Woodsy and the boy is beginning to be really worried himself. His balance has been affected, his vision remains blurred and the dizzy spells won't go away. Some mornings he comes into the ground and does a few laps but he cannot do any ball work because he just cannot handle that. The specialists have diagnosed a viral infection in his inner ear. That explains the balance problem and the dizziness and all the rest. But they don't know how it happened and they don't know when it will go away.

Nicky Walker who has now moved on to Hearts but was deputy for Chris Woods during his spell of illness.

I can see that it is getting Chris down. He is pretty low. All we can do is tell him to be patient but it is easier to say that than to do it. It must be terrible for Chris and for his family. He can't drive. He can't do so many ordinary things far less play football. The one positive step forward though is that the doctors could tell him what was wrong. He was starting to imagine all kinds of things before their diagnosis came through. Now he has to wait for the virus to disappear as suddenly as it arrived. That's the way the doctors think things will happen. One morning he will waken up and everything will be back to normal. I hope that comes soon to end the hell the lad is going through. There is so little we can do to help him. All we can offer is encouragement.

17 February 1989

Tomorrow Chris Woods will be back in goal for the first team. He has been missing since the middle of November. Altogether he has not played for us in our last 14 games. In that spell we have lost three games, have edged through to the second round of the Scottish Cup after another scare at Starks Park but have remained at the top of the League still leading the chase for the title. Chris has been tried in several reserve games, he has been training normally and there is a tremendous change in him. A weight has been lifted off his mind. Now he will be back and in the first team and he will be there on the run in to this title. The type of boy he is – he is a worrier – it was so much worse. It was a terrible personal test for him. The mental stress he had to live with and come through was enormous and now I think he will be a better man for that. I don't think there is any doubt about it.

Tomorrow it's the Cup, a home game against Stranraer and even with our Cup record that has to be the kind of fixture to allow Woodsy the chance to play himself back in. Let's hope so. It's important for the club. But, on this occasion, the club takes second place to the player – because it is vital for him. We are all rooting for him.

18 February 1989

No Cup jinx here. Nothing to worry us as we won 8-0 and the real bonus was having Chris Woods back in goal. Just to see him there was a boost to everyone at the club. And the fans gave him a huge welcome. They know how important he is and how important this next part of the season will be. To have him back for the run in was crucial. He is quality and he is one of the players I have whom I could sell for a lot of money simply by lifting the telephone. He is in that special category. Again, that's why he was given a new contract. He has an understanding with the back four and he is quite simply a superbly professional goalkeeper. He reads situations so well. His anticipation, his courage, his athleticism and, indeed, his very presence, single him out.

He is one of these keepers who fill the goal. You can get guys bigger than Chris who don't look as if they are going to stop you. But Woodsy does. When you are up against him and you are coming in on goal, you look up and you think to yourself: "God, these goals have shrunk". That's the way he fills that area. Shilton is the same. They make it hard for strikers just by the way they position themselves on their line. It's a secret that top keepers have. And it's important to them. His return will be inspirational for us. It can mean the difference between winning and losing the title. I know that deep down because I know how important a really top class keeper is to any team. He wins you games. He takes you through difficult days. And there are those kind of days ahead in the next few months.

19 April 1989

It has been a hard year for young Ian Durrant. He has had to sit it out since October watching us head towards the title, now seeing us qualify for the final of the Scottish Cup and seeing Scotland get closer and closer to Italy and the World Cup finals. He would have been involved so much in all of these competitions. Yet, because of injury he has been a spectator.

Now we have had to tell him that he needs another operation. There seems no end to the disappointments the lad has been forced to suffer. It is so unfair. He is back almost to square one and the hard work lies ahead of him again. We will have him back down to Lilleshall and hope that all the new developments, all the latest innovations in treatment, will pull him through. He seemed to be doing so well and then this set-back arrives.

Even though we are in the semi-final there's a cloud hanging over us because so many of the lads are thinking about Durrant. I know that I am and I think most of the other lads are the same. It is lousy luck and yet he still smiles and jokes his way through it all. If anyone deserves to get fit again and get playing again and get among the prizes he deserves, then it's him.

24 May 1989

Ian Durrant had his plaster removed last week and now he is starting back towards fitness. He was with us in Israel and he enjoyed himself with the rest of the lads as we all got over the disappointment of the Cup final defeat from Celtic. It is when you think how much the loss of Ian Durrant affected us that you wonder what we might have managed to achieve with him in the team. He has a long, hard road back but, as I have said all along, if anyone can do it then Durrant can.

It occurred all those months ago yet I still feel so angry, so hurt whenever I think about what happened to him. All that great, great promise being put on hold. It is a tragedy that he had to miss out on last season. All I want is to see him back in training. I'll be a happy man when that day comes along. I doubt if I would feel more elated the day Ian Durrant comes back than if it was myself returning from a bad injury.

More than anything else I just want to see him in the team again. We have missed him. I know he has missed out too. Terribly so. But the team lost something special when he was injured. An extraordinary player was lost to all of us – and to Scotland as well. I want him back for the team's sake, for his country's sake and for his own sake. The World Cup finals in Italy next summer would be the perfect stage for his talents. He would be a sensation there.

7

Into Europe . . . And Out Again

If there has been success in most competitions at home, there has been disappointment in Europe, that stage where Souness shone so often as a player. The success he had with Liverpool has still to rub off on Rangers. A quarter-final place in the European Cup is the best the Ibrox giants have achieved since Souness took over.

Last season they went out in the second round of the UEFA Cup to the West German Bundesliga side Cologne. Earlier they had beaten difficult opposition from Poland on yet another foray behind the Iron Curtain. Then, after the Skol Cup win, they were asked to travel to West Germany and only in the closing minutes did the skies fall in on them. It was then the damage was done and they found they could not repair it when the Germans came to Ibrox. European glory will always be a bonus to add to domestic success as far as Souness is concerned but he would like to make a mark in one of these star-studded tournaments, because he has made it clear – as David Murray has – that a European League is something which attracts him. It may not be too far off... .

6 September 1988

It was no great surprise to any of us when we were drawn to play behind the Iron Curtain again. This is our second trip to

131

Katowice in Poland and we have also been to Russia and Rumania since I arrived at Ibrox. It's no pleasure trip having to go into Eastern Europe. The flights are that bit longer, the food is not what you are used to – though we combat that by taking our own food with us as well as our own chef. It is the only way to do it. But we would still like to go with a substantial lead to Poland after tomorrow's first leg. It helps if you can travel with goals to back you in a hostile atmosphere. That has to be our aim tomorrow night even though we will be without Ally McCoist.

7 September 1988

Almost a full house saw us go through by just 1–0 with Mark Walters getting the all-important goal for us in the 73rd minute. It was a long time a-coming . . . and their time-wasting tactics infuriated the crowd and our players. John Brown got himself in trouble as he tried to hurry things along as their trainers defied the referee and the UEFA instructions about treating players on the field of play.

It was a frustrating night for all of us and the comfortable lead we looked for has not materialised. But I wonder just how good Katowice will be when they are asked to attack? It is interesting to think about that. Here all they did was defend and go down injured to waste time. When they have to come out to play us I doubt if they can match our all-round ability. There were few signs tonight that they could. I just hope I'm right because we would like to have a fair run in Europe this season. For the players' sake and also for the sake of the fans. They want European success and they want to see these games. The attendance of 41,120 proves that beyond any doubt. And, remember, the Poles are not the most attractive draw we might have got. The supporters knew what they could expect tonight.

5 October 1988

This was a special European performance from the team here tonight in the middle of the Polish coalfields. The players knew we were under the cosh before the game, defending a one-goal lead. Within a few minutes we found ourselves in worse shape.

Richard Gough shows the power in the air that European clubs fear – this is from a European tie against Cologne at Ibrox.

Their highly rated striker – he is on his way to play in West Germany – Furtok, snatched a goal after only four minutes. From that moment it became a test for us.

I have maintained for some time now that it can be easier to win away from home when teams open out than it often is when you are on your home ground. The lads proved my theory on the night. Big Terry Butcher was upfield for all the set pieces and scored two goals in a six-minute spell between 11 and 17 minutes. With the away goals counting double this put us in a very powerful position. But the players did not sit back and relax. When the Poles scored a second, our players upped a gear and Ian Durrant and Ian Ferguson helped themselves to a goal each to send us through to the second round of the UEFA Cup. That result gave us a convincing 5–2 aggregate and set us up for a crack at our next opponents. The draw is made on Friday and so we will learn then the quality of opposition we will be asked to face in the next round.

7 October 1988

No Iron Curtain trip this time, but a tough nut to crack in Cologne who are rated as one of the best teams in the West German Bundesliga. However, we can go to see them, we can learn about them and we can be better prepared for the two games than you can ever be for matches in the Eastern Bloc countries. I have a high regard for West German football. This will be a test. The worry for us is that we have qualified for the Skol Cup final and that falls on the Sunday before we have to play our first-leg tie in West Germany. That is something we could do without. I reckon we must be the only nation in Europe which would schedule a major Cup final the weekend before the European second-round ties are scheduled to be played.

25 October 1988

The Skol Cup is behind us. We won that. Now the next examination looms here in Cologne. They have a stack of experienced players, including the little veteran international Pierre Littbarski. We are without John Brown because he was suspended after the first-leg incident against the Poles. Other than that we can field more or less our Skol Cup-winning team.

A stylish Ally McCoist with his Crocodile Dundee hat alongside manager Souness.

We feel good and we reckon we can get a result even though there has to be some reaction after the Hampden game. The players would not be human if they were not affected in some way. We feel reasonably optimistic, however, because the team has been playing well and the first prize of the season is now on show in the Trophy Room at Ibrox.

26 October 1988

For 75 minutes we played the perfect European away leg in the Mungersdorff Stadium. The fans who had followed us there were the ones who were making the most noise in the 42,000 crowd. In the first half of the game Terry Butcher missed a chance. He volleyed one with his left foot which flew past. It surprised me because Terry has such a good left foot but there it was. A chance missed. Then Ally McCoist missed an absolute sitter which would have killed off the West Germans altogether. But we were getting so much of the ball, dominating so much of the game that it began to worry me.

I had said to Ray Wilkins at half-time that we had to try to avoid being pulled out too much and start to chase the game late on when all we might have to do was sit back a little and keep our discipline. Late in the game there were the ominous signs that this was happening. I have seen it happen before. Teams get that little bit confident and they start to try things, start to take little risks and what is looking to be a good result becomes a bad one. That is what happened to us. In 77 minutes they scored a spectacular goal and then a few minutes from the end we lost a second. A good enough goal, but I would always like to think that we could defend better than we did in that particular situation.

To compound the problems Ally McCoist became involved with one of their defenders and was sent off. So now we knew already that we had to face the second leg without two suspended players, Brown and McCoist, as well as our most effective European player, Ian Durrant. It is amazing what a dozen or so minutes can do to your plans in this game... .

8 November 1988

Things only seem to get worse. Ray Wilkins has been injured. With his experience he would have been important to us tomorrow night. On top of all the other worries it is a severe blow because we know that the Germans will be tight and they will be organised as only the Bundesliga teams can be.

We have to look for something early and then hope to put them under pressure with a little help from the crowd. The fans can be an important factor for us. But we have also to defend well because to allow them a goal would be to add to the suicidal mistakes we committed in the first-leg – or, at least, in the last quarter-of-an-hour of that match.

9 November 1988

We were forced to field Jimmy Nicholl tonight and also Davie Cooper, two players who have experience but whose best days are behind them. It was that or push young, almost untried players into a vital European tie. I wanted to avoid that.

We did not get the break we needed early in the game. The 42,204 fans were patient and they were willing us to win. There seemed to be a brief moment of hope when Kevin Drinkell scored in 75 minutes but, in the end, when we were desperately trying to put the game into extra-time they grabbed an equaliser. Europe was over for another year. And yet over the two games – especially if we had had a full team – I would have fancied us to beat them. Circumstances combined to knock us out this time. But we know that given a reasonable share of the breaks, and given the change to play our best side then we will get that long run in Europe that the fans want so much. Listen, we want it too... .

8

Another Championship Celebration

Graeme Souness has always maintained from the very day he took over at Ibrox that the League Championship is his major target EVERY season. His powerful belief that the team which wins the title is the best team in the land probably stems from his time with Liverpool when the Anfield men marched to so many title triumphs. He would like to end his Scottish Cup jinx. He would like to continue winning the Skol Cup. He would enjoy more success in Europe – this time as a manager rather than as a player. But, above all, he wants to win the title.

Last season saw him win the second Premier League Championship in the three years he has been at Ibrox. Clearly it delighted him. Not simply because it was another gong to celebrate in his short managerial career, but also because he knows the pressures placed on his players in the fiercely competitive Premier League. He recognises the demands made on the players at Ibrox.

Souness admits that he does not like the Premier League format. Playing each club four times is not to his liking – although he accepts that commercially the Top Ten set up has been an outstanding success. He has also grown to realise that as well as being competitive, the quality of play in the League is

as strong as it is in most European countries. That is why he takes
so much satisfaction from taking the title again.

Here he looks at some of the crucial fixtures the team played
and analyses some of the results. He also talks about some of the
players who were so important in the successes the team enjoyed
last season . . . including three wins over Celtic in the Old Firm
derby games. One of these, of course, came at Celtic Park where
Souness notched up his first-ever victory. That was a bonus,
perhaps, but over all it was the performances of the players week
in and week out which pleased the man at the top.

He asks a lot from his players but no more than he has asked
from himself throughout his career. It has paid off when you
look at the trophies he was won in his three years at Rangers –
two Championship trophies and three Skol Cups have been on
display in the Trophy Room at Ibrox in that time. It is a
managerial record anyone would be proud of.

12 August 1988

The season kicks off tomorrow and all I want is a decent
beginning so that we can start to lay last season's ghost as early
as possible. Everyone knows that this is the prize I want above
any other. The League to me always means that you have been
the best throughout the season. Other trophies mean other things
– in any Cup competition you can hit form on certain days, in
certain games – but if you are to take the title then you have to
be playing at or approaching your peak for 36 games. If you drop
your level of performance for any length of time then you won't
be champions. It is as simple as that for me. It is a long, hard
slog and no one can argue over the best team in the country at
the end of it because the best team is the one which finishes at
the top of the Premier League. The best team will be crowned
champions.

I know it is a cliché now but you really do have to take every
game one at a time. You can never afford to look too far ahead.
When you do that is when you slip up. Every game, after all,
throws up a different set of problems. You can look a few weeks
ahead and see a game which you think you will win easily and
then when you get there you find that injuries or illness or

suspensions have wrecked your team and suddenly the two points you were counting on are lost. Therefore the only way you can look at the League is by taking each game on its own merits.

27 August 1988

Celtic at Ibrox – the first big test. We slipped up a little last week already when we could only draw 0-0 at home to Hibs. After a winning start that was a disappointment to all of us. But I don't feel too bad because the team is playing good football – as good as they have played since I came here to be manager. Today's game is always one to be taken on its own – quite apart from the rest. It is a derby game of course, and they are always that bit different. But this one is unique. No one wants to make a mistake. Everyone is up for the match, the crowd is a sell out and the atmosphere is unbelievable.

Early on in my time as manager I was criticised because I said the game brought us only two points the same as any other. Some people took that to mean that I was downgrading the game's importance to the fans. It wasn't meant that way. I mean, it does bring just two points – but, also, I realise that the supporters want to see us win this one more than any other. I think that all the players know that too. And with Celtic coming as champions and as Cup-holders after that centenary season of success they enjoyed we have to prove ourselves here.

Like everyone else I look for this being a tight, tight game just as so many of them are. It turns out to be totally different and for 75 minutes we play exceptionally well. Strangely enough, we only do so after they have taken the lead in the first few minutes through Frank McAvennie. Fortunately, before they can settle in to that lead and maybe even capitalise on it, Coisty has equalised and we start to take over. We win 5-1 – a magnificent result. And it was one which contained several outstanding goals – particularly the second which came from Ray Wilkins. That had us leading at half-time and then McCoist, again, Kevin Drinkell and Mark Walters finished it all off. That was one of the special performances we have given in my time at Ibrox. I do spare a few thoughts for Ian Andrews who was making his Old Firm debut and who let in five goals. It was a difficult day for the lad and I'm sure he will get over it given time. He will probably be a better player once he can push away the memories of today.

27 September 1988

Another of our very professional performances tonight. This is our sixth win out of our first seven games and Ian Ferguson is the player who scores against Dundee United at Tannadice. Only seven minutes are left when he gets the goal – and it's a good one. As well as racking up victories we have been able to do so while losing just three goals in seven games and Hibs are the one team to have taken a point from us. There is a refreshing zest about the team just now and, mainly, we have been able to put out a settled looking side in almost all of the games. The constant chopping and changing, the adjustments which had to be made all the way through last season, have gone now. I always felt reasonably confident that if we could get that settled formation then we would be able to show our best form and that is turning out to be true.

This, with the Celtic result, is a very important one for the team. OK, it's only another two points but they have been earned against another team whom we would expect to shape up as genuine contenders for the title. That is one thing you can look ahead to and assess – the teams who will be challenging at the top. You always look for Celtic, Aberdeen and Dundee United to be in the pack at the top. We have played two of them and taken full points – Aberdeen loom ahead in ten days' time.

8 October 1988

It's another test this afternoon, playing Aberdeen at Pittodrie in a game where they have made it plain that they have to stop us. All the pre-match noises from their camp are about stopping us running away with the title. I don't know where that kind of talk can come from because we have played only eight games. This is us now reaching the quarter stage of the season. How can anyone think of the championship just now? I know that we are not and if anyone talked title in the dressing-room I would have a few words to say to them. It's daft to talk that way when you have 28 games left to play. Even if we were to win today I wouldn't be thinking about being champions.

In the end we don't win. We lose 2–1 but the result isn't the main worry because Ian Durrant has been carried off and things look bad for him. Sometimes when you get a young, talented player injured badly like this then you stop bothering about the result of the game. When I saw Durrant in the dressing-room the game became an irrelevance. We will have to pick up for our midweek match at Easter Road but right now no one is thinking about that.

10 October 1988

The Durrant injury is a blow to the boy and a blow to the team now that we know how long he is going to be out. We were playing with so much confidence mainly because we had stayed clear of injury – apart from the knock Ian Ferguson took in the pre-season clash with Bordeaux. That led to a continuity of selection and it's from that kind of continuity that good results and good performances spring. I always feel that if I can get my best 14 or 15 players operating every week then we are in with a shout for anything. It is when injuries start to bite into you that you get the real problems and we have had more than our fair share, I would reckon.

Until now, a quarter of the way through the League programme, I have been delighted with all the players. But maybe Mark Walters has taken the eye a little more than the others because he is that kind of entertaining player. He is one that fans turn out to watch. And it's been great to see Terry Butcher back because it was not only his ability we missed at the heart of the defence for so much of last season, it was his very presence. It was his leadership. He is inspirational and he is a tremendous captain because he commands the respect of other players. I don't think a captain has to bark at other players. You can get respect in other ways – by example mainly, I suppose – and Terry has that special presence about him, that professionalism and that winning streak which makes everyone in the side look up to him. When I captained Liverpool I knew that I could not play well in every game and so I used to actively encourage people to give me abuse on the field if I wasn't doing the business. That happens here. If Terry drops a bit then we have players who can give him a little bit of stick. It is the way it should be – but already, after just these nine League games, we know just how much we missed the big fellow last season. If anyone else wondered how important he was to us then they only have to look at the differences between last season and this one so far. Touch wood nothing happens to change that.

12 November 1988

The second Old Firm game of the season – and it would be good if we could get a result today. A victory, I mean, because it does annoy me that since I arrived in Scotland to manage Rangers we have not been able to win at Parkhead. It's a problem which was here with the club before my coming, too. Our Premier League record at their ground is not good. It would be a little bit special if we were able to improve on it today.

But that's not the way it turns out. Instead, while we take the lead through a Mark Walters' penalty in the 18th minute, they go on to take both points with a little bit of help from big Terry who scores a spectacular own goal which does help bring them back into the game. So much so that they are 3–1 up at half-time and that is the way the game stays. I cannot believe that we lost this one and I cannot believe the number of goals scored in the two matches so far this season between ourselves and Celtic. I always thought these were tight games, with 1–0 or 0–0 or 1–1 or whatever being the likeliest results. Two games have brought TEN goals. This is not normal derby day scoring.

14 November 1988

We have had bad news about Chris Woods, and Ally McCoist is out. So the rhythm we hoped to keep, the continuity in selection we were looking for, has gone. That means, along with wee Ian Durrant, that we have three top men out. This midweek we have Hamilton, then we travel to Dens Park and then we have

Mark Walters celebrates after setting up another goal for one of his Rangers' team-mates.

Aberdeen at home. The Celtic game must not be the start of any major slip-up by us. We cannot afford that, although it's when the team is disrupted you start to look for problems arriving. Surely we have had enough? Surely a trio of international players out of action is more than any team deserves to look for during a season? You would hope so... .

26 November 1988

Another point lost at Dundee when we also had Mark Walters and Neale Cooper out of the side as well as the other three. Davie Cooper was drafted back in and Jimmy Nicholl was on the bench. It's all a bit of a nightmare again but at least Mark and Neale Cooper are back for this one against Aberdeen. It's one we want to win and we do. Richard Gough gets the goal just before half-time and that one goal is enough to give us the two points we so desperately wanted – and so desperately needed – from this crunch game. When Goughie gets a goal you can usually assume it will be an important one. This was no exception. It is a very satisfying result.

3 December 1988

Just a week ago we were being all self-congratulatory. This afternoon we were brought back to earth with a thump. Dundee United came to our place, managed one shot at goal and they scored. Kevin Gallacher set up the chance – and we were caught chasing the game. He gets the ball over from the left and Dave Beaumont is there to score. We had players out of position and that should not have happened. Thirteen minutes left and we are caught looking for a win – and because of that allowing United the space to snatch victory for themselves. It is a blow and it is also a lesson. It would have been far better for us to have kept our discipline and lost the one point only, rather than risk exposing ourselves so late and in doing so lose a goal. It is a result which makes me angry. United have a habit of coming into games late and stealing a result. We should have been more aware of that. I thought we were more aware of that. It drives home the lesson that you can never relax in this Premier League.

More from the Premier League – and old team-mates Richard Gough and Dundee United's Paul Hegarty joust in the air.

10 December 1988

The changes we are being forced to make and the loss of key players is affecting us now. At Tynecastle today, against a team we had beaten three times already this season, we went down 2–0. It was a bad result which culminated with a defensive mix-up which allowed Iain Ferguson to get their late second goal. There is little we can do about the players who are out through long-term injuries – but we have to restore our earlier attitude. The little slide cannot continue. We stopped it successfully after the defeat from Celtic and bounced back with a win over Aberdeen. Now we have a chance again next week to do something. Hibs, who took a point from us in the second game of the season, return to Ibrox. Let's hope we get back to our winning ways... .

3 January 1989

Hibs and Hamilton are behind us. Four points were taken and now it's back to the Old Firm. We have to win to stop them catching up too much on us at the top. They must see this as an opportunity to bite into our lead. But we cannot allow that to happen. The big three remain out but Derek Ferguson is back and the two recent results have helped put some confidence back into the side.

But Celtic are the team whose confidence goes sky high after only a minute. That's how long it takes Chris Morris to score and have their fans singing. But as in the other Old Firm games this season the team which scores first doesn't go on to win. We take over. Terry Butcher scores. Mark Walters gets another with a penalty and right on half-time Ian Ferguson gives us a 3–1 lead. Before the end Mark adds another – and that gives him four goals so far this season against Celtic.

It was another remarkable match and while they missed Frank McAvennie who had to go off injured in the first half, we played very well once again. It was quite an event and the goals tally was high again. The three games have now brought a total of 15 goals. You would normally be lucky to get that in two whole seasons! It is a very important result psychologically and with Aberdeen and Dundee United drawing, it gives us an edge at a time when all three of the other teams at the top might have

Opponents then – and opponents again today, for both Jimmy Nicholl, then at Ibrox, and Mo Johnston, then with Celtic, have switched clubs. Nicholl is with Dunfermline and Mo is one of the new Rangers idols.

thought of making up ground on us. It didn't happen that way and maybe now we can recapture some of the form we showed so often in the early stages of the season. Certainly I'd like to think we can.

7 January 1989

No winning streak at all. Just a miserable performance from exactly the same players who defeated Celtic. Now at Fir Park we lose to Motherwell. Too many players seem to have been carried away by the fact that we were able to win against Celtic and win again well. So they take that as a signal to relax. They have to get it into their heads that you don't relax. Not at all. Because if you do then you get caught. Just the way we were caught today.

Possibly the fact that we scored first after just 20 minutes when Kevin Drinkell got the goal didn't help our attitude problem. We possibly thought it was going to be another win and we took our foot off the accelerator. When Motherwell scored through Fraser Wishart immediately the second half started we found we could not raise our game to the right level again. An own goal by Goughie finished us.

I was angry and the players knew it. All the good they did themselves last week has been undone. But the worst thing I have to accept is that it happened because of a degree of unprofessionalism in the performance – something we lecture the players about constantly. Sometimes you wonder if they listen to you. Sometimes you wonder just how often you have to repeat the same things over and over again. Then, there are the good times too. The times when you realise that they HAVE listened and the times when things come off just as you tell them they will. I suppose they balance out. But this is a low point of the season – mainly, I suppose, because we hit one of our highs at the beginning of the week. You think you are starting the New Year in style and Motherwell, a team fighting relegation, haul the rug away. To compound it, the other three at the top all win. When things go wrong in this game then they really do go totally wrong. Next week we are away to Aberdeen. Interesting.

Terry Butcher finishes on top in this tussle with one-time Celtic striker Frank McAvennie.

14 January 1989

A return to Pittodrie and this time we are able to come back with a win which strengthens our grip at the top of the Premier League. We make a little tactical switch here which works for us. Big John Brown drops into the full-back slot and we push Stuart Munro forward. He does so well for us getting up that left flank and tying down their full-back, Stewart McKimmie. Young Derek Ferguson gets the goals – though Stuart Munro does put in a claim on one of them. At the end of the day no one is going to argue too much. It is a valuable win and it's another which has been achieved without those three key players. I don't think any other team in Scotland could have handled this handicap as well as we have – and maybe only one or two in England. If any. Apart from the odd lapse the lads have kept at it well. We all know that when we start seeing the injuries clear then we can only get better. It is a nice thought.

1 April 1989

The last Old Firm game of the season – and we know that this is going to be a vital one again. That result at Aberdeen has set us off on the kind of run which wins titles when they happen at this stage of a season. Even though we still ban title talk you can't help realising that it is coming closer and closer with every game we play. And every game we win. Apart from the loss of one point at Tannadice – more of that in a moment – we have now won FIVE games since losing at Motherwell. It has been impressive and might have been more so but for the one draw against Dundee United. We had led through a Stuart Munro goal in the first-half and the game was in injury time when Gary Stevens put the ball into his own net. It was an accident and it could have been avoided and, in any case, the referee had played over the 90 minutes. It was a blow to us because we had played well enough to win and we deserved to get the points. However, going there and returning with even one point was acceptable. All that bothered us was the way the point had been lost.

All in all, though, we could not have given ourselves a better launching pad than that string of results as we get ready for the game at Parkhead. Celtic have pushed themselves back into

Aerial challenge! Giant Rangers' skipper Terry Butcher rises above Aberdeen centre-half Alex McLeish who has Kevin Drinkell behind him.

contention – as I knew they would – but, again, they MUST win today if they are to have a chance at all of taking the flag.

We were two goals up in half an hour with a goal from Kevin Drinkell putting us in front after only five minutes and then another from Ally McCoist putting us in command for the rest of that half. Andy Walker snatched one back for them very quickly after the game restarted in the second half and they had a good spell then. But, in the end, we won. It was good to get a result there on a personal level. But it was also good because this must have been the day when we sickened the others who were still chasing us. Especially Aberdeen. They managed to beat Dundee United by 1–0 but any joy they had from that must have evaporated when the news of our result hit them. They must have looked at us going to Parkhead and thought it was a day when they could put us under severe pressure. It turned out the other way.

This was a decisive day as far as the title is concerned and I'm sure that EVERYONE, but EVERYONE, from Aberdeen right down through the whole country will realise it. It has been important and it has been highly satisfying as well. Laying any jinx – such as the one which seemed to hit me at Parkhead – is always good. I only hope that if this is to be the season when hoodoos end the Cup one which also dogs my career will vanish too. Maybe that's asking for too much. One thing at a time will do.

At this stage I think we all know that if the worst comes to the worst then it will be a title shoot-out with Aberdeen in the last game of the season. If we suffer any setbacks or any disappointments then we will still have the chance to rectify them when Aberdeen have to come to Ibrox. If it goes to that then I'm confident that we have the players who will be able to handle that type of situation. I'm sure that we will handle that one if it becomes necessary. There are a few trip-wires waiting for us which we will have to avoid. Like Paisley in a couple of weeks. That's never a happy hunting ground for us. Never has been in my time at Ibrox and it was an 87th minute goal from Andy Gray which gave us a draw there at Love Street earlier this season. I don't want to suffer that kind of agony again. Not now. Not at this time of the season.

The Hibs' defence is in tatters as Kevin Drinkell powers a shot towards goal with Ian Ferguson looking on anxiously.

22 April 1989

This is the one I worried about, though Motherwell made us sweat a bit at Ibrox after the Celtic game. The way they play will get the game stopped. All they want to do is defend. I doubt if I would pay to watch them. Not doing what they do against us at any rate. The lads are right for this one at Paisley. You get that feeling in the dressing-room. The end is coming that little bit closer and they don't want to let anyone down now.

They don't either. Ian Ferguson scores another great goal before half-time and then Coisty finishes things off with a header. That sealed the game. We played well. We missed a few chances and that was the only worry I had sitting there watching. When you miss scoring opportunities and you are only a goal ahead you begin to worry that the opposition will slip back in. But we were too professional this time. As I said, you could sense the feeling in the dressing-room before the players went out. The best bonus of all, though, came with the news from Tynecastle where Hearts have beaten Aberdeen. Now we know exactly what is needed. If we can beat Hearts at Ibrox next week we will win the League. The title will be back at Ibrox. What a good day this has been.

29 April 1989

There was only going to be one result in this one. You sit there as a manager watching games and there are some when you know that everything is going to be all right after seeing the first five minutes. This was one of these. The semi-final replay against St Johnstone was another. You get them through the season but it's nice to have one when the championship is about to be settled. This is the day, after all, when a whole season's efforts are rewarded. But in these opening minutes I know nothing can possibly go wrong. Nothing will stop the celebrations. We were in business from the beginning. Mel Sterland helped himself to two goals and Kevin Drinkell grabbed another two. Mel took his before half-time, Kevin added his in the second-half. And that was it. Now it didn't matter what anyone else did.

A determined Ian Ferguson tracks Gary Lineker of Spurs.

It really summed up what we have been preaching to the players all the way through the season. If you do your own job right then no one will be able to beat you to the title. You don't rely on others – do it yourself. At the end that is what we did today and how the crowd enjoyed it. How we all enjoyed it! Every single one of us. This is what the game is all about. Days like this one. They stick with you forever no matter how many times you might win a trophy. You don't forget any of them because every one of them means something special. I tell the players that – "Savour this, because no one can ever take it away from you!"

30 April 1989

A little bit of time for reflection, and the fact that we were able to take six points out of eight from Celtic certainly helped us to win the title. But then we also had to take valuable points at Tannadice and at Pittodrie to make sure we were champions. It is too easy to say that winning the bulk of the Old Firm games can make you champions. The last two years it has perhaps worked out that way – but I don't think you would find Aberdeen, Dundee United, Hearts and Hibs subscribing to the theory that whichever one of the two Glasgow clubs come out on top will be champions. Mind you, it does help the cause – and it keeps the supporters happy if you do put one over on your rivals in an Old Firm clash. You had better believe that!

Winning the Premier League is extremely difficult. The fact that you have to play every club four times makes it that way. And in my view it makes it even more difficult for ourselves and Celtic. Rival clubs and rival fans won't agree. They will say that we are the Big Two and therefore we can buy players that other clubs can't buy and therefore we have it easy. It is not the case. The four-match-a-season situation is one which does not always suit us because it allows the lesser clubs to get to know the better players in the League – and I'm not talking simply about my own club here – and then work out ways to stop these quality players. Stopping someone is always that bit easier than going out to create something yourself. Everyone knows that. But if you play

Richard Gough came home to look for honours. Here he clut-ches one of those he has won with Rangers – the League Championship Trophy.

someone four times – and that could be more, adding in Cup games – then you find out ways to make life difficult. I don't know if that is good for the game.

I know that the Premier League is a healthy one as far as gates are concerned. The attendances have been amazing and the Premier League is one of the success stories of Europe as far as that goes. But I believe if you ask anyone in the game, players or managers or coaches, then they would all agree with me that it is not healthy as far as the playing side is concerned. In fact, while it has been a success so far, I think that will change. I think the fans will grow fed up with it.

It's not ideal, but maybe you cannot achieve the ideal and as far as the economic side of the game is concerned then the Premier League set up is right for Scotland. I just find it hard to adjust to – as I'm sure most players have done – because I grew up in a League where you played the opposition just twice in a season. Still, we have to get on with the League as it is and win it as it is constructed. No matter how difficult it might be. Any title is hard to win – this one is just that bit harder when you are one of the teams everyone is trying to shoot down. And we are always going to be one of them. We all know that.

The top teams in the Premier League are the match for top teams in most of the leagues in Europe and the quality extends further down the table, too. Hearts are a team who impress me and their League position at the end of season 1988–89 was not a reflection on their ability as a team. The way they played in Europe and the successes they had there give a better idea of their capabilities. I like the way they give 100 per cent effort from the first minute to the last minute. Hibs, too, have impressed me. They try to play a bit more football than Hearts do. They are more technical in their approach and they have young players they hope will mature. John Collins and Paul Kane are two of them. But the teams with the obvious threat are those who seem always to finish in the top four in the table. Aberdeen have a lot of experience which has brought them years of success and they pose a threat every season. Dundee United are the same. Again they have experience in there and the players with that experience have tasted success and are familiar with the demands made by

Celebrating the Championship win and young Tom Cowan, in the middle of this group, gets a taste of glory. Other players are, left to right, Ian Ferguson, Derek Ferguson, Mark Walters, Chris Woods and Terry Butcher.

the Premier League set up. Celtic, too, have that experience and several outstanding players – the most exceptional being Paul McStay, of course.

My team have to be on their toes, they have to be prepared to face these challenges and they can do that only by being 100 per cent ready all the time. If they go on to that field one per cent down then they will struggle. There is no room for players who don't fancy the challenge. Or the pressure.

In season 1989–90 I hope to be in the position that Bob Paisley used to be in at Anfield. I want to have another couple of quality players in the squad and then I won't have to shout and bawl so much. I won't have to lose my temper with players who allow their standards to drop or their concentration to lapse or their hunger to fade. My actions will speak for me. Non-fanciers, as we used to call players who don't relish the battle every week, will be out. They will go. The players I want are those who are up every week. Those who can scarcely wait for the whistle to blow in every game. We have a hard core of that type of professional in the squad now. I want more. Our club MUST have players with the truly professional attitude. When I went to Liverpool I didn't have that. It was not an attitude I had when I was a young player. I learned it there at Anfield and within 12 months I knew what they wanted and I accepted it. If I hadn't then I would have been on my bike. It is as simple as that.

It is all about being a good professional. You cannot pick your games when you are with a club like Rangers. You cannot go on to the field expecting to take it easy in some matches and then turn it on in others. That won't do. It has to be 100 per cent all the time.

All I am aiming for now is to give the fans – who are the best in the business – a team they will enjoy watching. And give them the trophies they expect this club to win. Just as the players cannot drop their standards, I cannot drop mine as a manager either. The support expects the best. My job is to give them that. And I feel we are on the right road. A couple more players, if I can get them, will push us still closer to my ideal squad. Then watch us go... .

1988/89 SEASON

The Skol Cup – Round by Round

Second Round
Wednesday August 17

CLYDE 0   RANGERS 3
                           Drinkell (17)
                           Walters (39)
                           Ferguson D (84)   Att 19,000

Third Round
Wednesday August 24

RANGERS 6   CLYDEBANK 0
McCoist (9)
Gough (26)
Walters (37)
Wilkins (58)
Drinkell (71)
Durrant (89)   Att 34,256

Semi-final
Wednesday September 21

RANGERS 3   HEARTS 0
Walters (11, 88)   At Hampden
Nisbet (53)   Att 53,623

Final
Sunday October 23

RANGERS 3   ABERDEEN 2
McCoist (15, pen 88)   Dodds (20, 62)   At Hampden
Ferguson I (55)   Att 72,123

Rangers' Premier Division Record

DATE		H/A	RES	ATT	SCORERS (MINS)
Aug 13	Hamilton	A	2–0	10,500	Stevens (44), McCoist (65)
Aug 20	Hibernian	H	0–0	41,850	
Aug 27	Celtic	H	5–1	44,000	McCoist (10, 46), Wilkins (36), Drinkell (59), Walters (63)
Sep 3	Motherwell	A	2–0	20,112	Drinkell (26), Durrant (34)
Sep 17	Hearts	A	2–1	23,401	Durrant (47 pen), Nisbet (65)
Sep 24	St Mirren	H	2–1	35,523	Cooper D (61 pen), Walters (68)
Sep 27	Dundee Utd	A	1–0	20,071	Ferguson I (83)
Oct 1	Dundee	H	2–0	40,768	Drinkell (11), Walters (85)
Oct 8	Aberdeen	A	1–2	23,000	Cooper N (39)
Oct 12	Hibernian	A	1–0	27,000	McCoist (27)
Oct 29	St Mirren	A	1–1	20,903	Gray (87)
Nov 1	Hearts	H	3–0	36,505	Gough (56), Walters (64 pen), Gray (79)
Nov 5	Motherwell	H	2–1	38,060	Brown (18), Drinkell (90)
Nov 12	Celtic	A	1–3	60,113	Walters (18 pen)
Nov 16	Hamilton	H	3–1	36,864	Gray (43), Ferguson I (52), Drinkell (83)
Nov 19	Dundee	A	0–0	16,514	
Nov 26	Aberdeen	H	1–0	42,239	Gough (43)
Dec 3	Dundee Utd	H	0–1	39,200	
Dec 10	Hearts	A	0–2	26,424	
Dec 17	Hibernian	H	1–0	36,672	McCoist (66)
Dec 31	Hamilton	A	1–0	10,500	Ferguson D (75)
Jan 3	Celtic	H	4–1	42,515	Butcher (16), Walters (20 pen), Ferguson I (45)

Jan	7	Motherwell	A	1–2	19,275	Drinkell (21)
Jan	14	Aberdeen	A	2–1	23,000	Ferguson D (11, 23)
Jan	21	Dundee	H	3–1	43,202	Ferguson I (38), Butcher (49), McCoist (86)
Feb	11	Dundee Utd	A	1–1	22,013	Munro (39)
Feb	25	St Mirren	H	3–1	39,021	Ferguson I (18), McCoist (75), Walters (78)
Mar	11	Hamilton	H	3–0	35,733	Ferguson I (46), Sterland (75), Gough (89)
Mar	25	Hibernian	A	1–0	22,000	Drinkell (42)
Apr	1	Celtic	A	2–1	60,171	Drinkell (5), McCoist (32)
Apr	8	Motherwell	H	1–0	37,782	McCoist (59)
Apr	22	St Mirren	A	2–0	21,413	Ferguson I (40), McCoist (85)
Apr	29	Hearts	H	4–0	42,856	Sterland (17, 40), Drinkell (57, 70)
May	2	Dundee Utd	H	2–0	39,058	Drinkell (16), McCoist (34)
May	6	Dundee	A	2–1	14,889	Gray (66, 75)
May	13	Aberdeen	H	0–3	42,480	

Biggest Home Win: 5–1 v Celtic, Aug 27
Biggest Away Win: 2–0 v Hamilton, Aug 13
                     v Motherwell, Sept 3
                     v St Mirren, April 22
Biggest Home Defeat: 0–3 v Aberdeen, May 13
Biggest Away Defeat: 1–3 v Celtic, November 12

Most goals in a game: 2 – Ally McCoist v Celtic, August 27
                        Mark Walters v Celtic, January 3
                        Derek Ferguson v Aberdeen, Jan 14
                        Mel Sterland and Kevin Drinkell v Hearts, April 29
                        Andy Gray v Dundee, May 6

How They Finished

		P	W	D	L	F	A	W	D	L	F	A	PTS
1.	Rangers	36	15	1	2	39	11	11	3	4	23	15	**56**
2.	Aberdeen	36	10	7	1	26	10	8	7	3	25	15	**50**
3.	Celtic	36	13	1	4	35	18	8	3	7	31	26	**46**
4.	Dundee Utd	36	6	8	4	20	16	10	4	4	24	10	**44**
5.	Hibernian	36	8	4	6	20	16	5	5	8	17	20	**35**
6.	Hearts	36	7	6	5	22	17	2	7	9	13	25	**31**
7.	St Mirren	36	5	6	7	17	19	6	1	11	22	36	**29**
8.	Dundee	36	8	4	6	22	21	1	6	11	12	27	**28**
9.	Motherwell	36	5	7	6	21	21	2	6	10	14	23	**27**
10.	Hamilton	36	5	0	13	9	42	1	2	16	10	34	**14**

Scottish Cup – Round by Round

Third Round
Saturday January 28

RAITH ROVERS 1	RANGERS 1	
Dalziell (53)	Ferguson I (67)	Att 10,500

Third Round Replay
Wednesday February 1

RANGERS 3	RAITH ROVERS 0	
Walters (34)		
Drinkell (47)		
Fraser (o.g. 79)		Att 40,307

Fouth Round
Saturday February 18

RANGERS 8	STRANRAER 0	
Ferguson I (11)		
Drinkell (33, 47)		
Brown (35)		
McCoist (pen 36, 37)		
Walters (38)		
Butcher (44)		Att 41,198

Quarter-final
Saturday March 18

RANGERS 2   DUNDEE UNITED 2
Drinkell (52)   Gallacher (18)
McCoist (69)   Paatelainen (81)   Att 42,177

Quarter-final Replay
Monday March 27

DUNDEE UNITED 0   RANGERS 1
                        McCoist (49)   Att 21,872

Semi-final
Saturday April 15

RANGERS 0   ST JOHNSTONE 0   Att 42,374

Semi-final Replay
Tuesday April 18

ST JOHNSTONE 0   RANGERS 4
                        Walters (43),
                        Stevens (44),
                        Drinkell (45),
                        McCoist (63)   Att 44,256

Final
Saturday May 13

CELTIC 1   RANGERS 0   At Hampden
Miller (42)   Park
                                                Att 72,059

Scottish Clubs in Europe

Wednesday September 7
UEFA Cup – First Round First Leg

RANGERS 1   KATOWICE 0
Walters (73)   Att 41,120

Wednesday October 5
UEFA Cup – First Round Second Leg

KATOWICE 2   RANGERS 4
Furtok (4)   Butcher (11, 17)
Kubisztla (63)   Durrant (71)
                        Ferguson I (78)
(Rangers won 5–2 on aggregate)   Att 40,000

Wednesday October 26
UEFA Cup – Second Round First Leg

COLOGNE 2   RANGERS 0
Janssen (77)
Allofs (87)   Att 42,000

Wednesday November 9
UEFA Cup – Second Round Second Leg

RANGERS 1   COLOGNE 1
Drinkell (75)   Janssen (90)
(Cologne won 3–1 on aggregate)   Att 42,204